BURPEE

AMERICAN GARDENING SERIES

CUTTING GARDENS

Chet Davis

Prentice Hall Gardening
New York • London • Toronto • Sydney • Tokyo • Singapore

PRENTICE HALL GENERAL REFERENCE
15 Columbus Circle
New York, New York, 10023

Library of Congress Cataloging-in-Publication data

Davis, Chet.
    Cutting gardens / Chet Davis.
        p.   cm.—(Burpee American gardening series)
    Includes index.
    ISBN 0-671-85043-1
    1. Flower gardening.   2. Cut flowers.   3. Flowers.   I. Title.
    II. Series.
    SB405.D295   1994
    635.9'66—dc20   92-41054
                                                              CIP

Manufactured in the United States of America

10   9   8   7   6   5   4   3   2   1

First Edition

There are very few opportunities in life in which to declare one's undying gratitude for all of a person's support and belief; I dedicate this book to Mary, my partner, wife, and personal cheer-leading squad.

There are many others who deserve credit for the wonderful efforts on behalf of this book. To Suzie Bales, who felt I might know enough words and be able to put them down in a cohesive manner, and then held my hand as paranoia struck while expressing my words eloquently in her photography. To Gina Norgard, photo-shoot designer, who helped put each flower arrangement in its best light. To Martha Kraska, gardener extraordinaire, who provided all the right flowers and at the right time. Thank you.

To all the folks at Prentice Hall, but specifically Rebecca Atwater, who made it all come together and whose talent with a pad of memo flags and a red pencil made my words flow. To Rachel Simon, who made every detail count.

Finally, to everyone at Mohonk Mountain House, my home for the past ten years. To the dedicated gardeners and talented florists who make the beauty at Mohonk. And to the Smiley family, who continue to support the floral endeavors at Mohonk and who make Mohonk Magic come true. Thank you.

Photo Credits:

Agricultural Research Service, USDA: 92–93; *Armitage, Allan:* page 59 top; *Ball Seed Co.:* page 57 top; *Dirr, Michael:* page 63 top; *Druse, Ken:* pages 66, 73 bottom; *Floranova Ltd:* page 56 bottom; *Gitts, Nicholas, of Swan Island Dahlias:* page 79 middle; *Horticultural Photography, Corvallis, OR:* 74 left; *Mohonk Mountain House Archives:* page 24; *Netherlands Flower Bulb Information Center:* pages 77 bottom, 78 bottom, 79 bottom; *PanAmerican Seed Co.:* page 54 right; *Rokach, Allen:* page 62 bottom; *Sakata Seed America, Inc.:* page 51 bottom; *Viette, Andre:* page 69 bottom; *W. Atlee Burpee & Co.:* pages 46 top left and bottom, 47 both, 48 both, 49 top, 50 top, 52 bottom, 53 both, 54 left, 58 both, 59 bottom, 60 middle and bottom, 63 bottom, 67 bottom left, 68 top and middle, 71 top and middle, 75, 76 left, 77 top, 81 both, 83 both.

Illustrations on pages 12, 15, 19, 21, 25, 26 and 32 by Elayne Sears

Illustrations on page 22 by Michael Gale

On the cover: Garden roses are harvested and ready to be brought indoors where their fragrance and beauty will be enjoyed for days to come. Fresh flowers do so much to enhance our lives, and can complement any decor and occasion. Preceding pages: The Show Garden at Mohonk Mountain House in New Paltz, New York. This historic garden provides inspiration for flower arrangers, photographers and artists, as well as some flowers for cutting.

CONTENTS

INTRODUCTION

Flowers in the home are one of those little niceties we can provide for ourselves. The accent of color and scent do much to lift the spirits when avid gardeners find themselves indoors. A flower arrangement need be neither large nor elaborate to be wonderfully effective. I hope to share the enjoyment of the cutting garden experience and to discourage the floral enthusiast from getting bogged down in the virtually endless list of floral design rules and regulations with which we seem to have been burdened since Queen Victoria first started tightening her corset laces. These rules are like rules in cooking, painting or any other hobby; they help the novice learn the basics, but after that, it's best to relax and enjoy creating beauty.

Plants suitable for cutting represent all the major groups of ornamental plants: herbaceous annuals, perennials, biennials, woody trees, shrubs, vines and groundcovers. But why stop there? Stretch the imagination and use wildflowers, weeds, culinary and aromatic herbs and vegetables to create delightfully unique decorations. This book is designed to lead you through the process of creating a cutting garden suitable for your landscape, and to help you plant, grow and harvest (yes, harvest!) materials suitable for a variety of arrangements. For many, the cutting of flowers for arrangements offers a feeling of accomplishment similar to that we may get when harvesting peas, tomatoes and other edibles. A sense of well-being, bounty and—let's not forget—cost savings. Flowers harvested from the garden are as fresh as you will ever find, and they allow you to express yourself in colors, textures and fragrances of your choosing. They let you bring the outdoors in.

The avid horticulturist will learn from the cutting garden. For example, nuances of color in the petals will become more evident when seen from the perspective of the dining table or desktop, and plants successfully combined in the vase may later be similarly grouped in the garden bed. In this way the vase can become a sort of laboratory for the garden. The wily gardener need not laboriously move plants around in the garden to try variations of textures, colors and forms. The cutting garden and flower arrangement become tools you can use to learn more about plants and your garden. This book offers pointers on design. The elements of good design, involving color, texture, balance, rhythm and proportion, are all easily practiced in the vase.

Over the years the cutting gardens at Mohonk Mountain House, where I garden, have provided me with great pleasure. There, tremendous numbers of cut flowers nurtured by dedicated gardeners are harvested and beautifully arranged by talented florists. Flower bouquets on a grand scale grace the hallways of this historic, venerable mountaintop retreat. Displays of this sort have impressed generations of guests seeking to revive their spirits.

All garden endeavors require some study and planning. The chapters that follow will help you create a basic garden plan that will yield cut flowers and greens for your arrangements. More than a paint-by-numbers approach, my advice aims to broaden your horizons by helping you look at a plant's flowers and leaves in a new light. Novice gardeners will learn the essentials of planting as well as how to nurture and harvest the bounty of their labors; old-timers may pick up some tips to improve the use of their landscapes, and I hope they will be introduced to some new plants and techniques along the way.

A word for the faint at heart: Frequently when cutting flowers from the garden, I will hear a low groan—not from the plant being cut, but from an onlooker. Some people seem to harbor a sensitivity to "hurting" the plants. In fact, most plants benefit from cutting. The plants frequently produce more blossoms or succulent shoots, becoming denser and stronger for their sacrifice. Nor is cutting from the garden a sacrifice of blooms. Plant materials harvested and properly handled will frequently outlast their garden counterparts as they are not exposed to wind, rain, insects and disease. Once in the vase, the flowers and greens can successfully live out their lives in regal splendor.

Daffodils harvested from a naturalized planting find a home in a crockery vase.
Buds of Amelachier, *and hemlock and hosta foliage complete the composition.*

THE CUTTING GARDEN PLANNER

CHOOSING PLANTS FOR THE CUTTING GARDEN

The plants you choose will have to be harvested to be enjoyed in the house. They must be able to last when placed in water. The plant portraits (page 45) recommend those varieties best for cutting. Quite simply, those that don't last in water are not suitable for cutting, although they may be enjoyed in many other ways, including for their garden beauty and fragrance, in potpourri or garden crafts, as edible flowers and as pretty garnishes.

Ages ago, some brilliant person created order in the garden by classifying plants in groups, each group planted in a different part of the garden. Over the years these artificial plant groupings have been maintained as if written in stone. Therefore, we have perennial borders, annual borders, herb gardens, vegetable gardens and shrubbery borders. Later you'll see I'm not averse to anarchy in the garden; we'll overthrow these artificial plant groupings and create gardens to serve a specific purpose.

Plants are grouped by botanical type; thus we speak of annuals, biennials, herbaceous perennials and woody perennials. Within these categories we find our familiar friends: flowers, trees, shrubs, herbs, vegetables and so on. Annuals, frequently grown from seed, complete their life cycle in one year. However, in the annual group of plants, some perennials and biennials are often included. Confused? For practical reasons some perennials native to warm areas and unable to survive cold winter climates are treated as annuals. In a warmer climate, they may be content in the garden for many years. An example of a tropical perennial is the familiar coleus; another, the common horticultural geranium (*Pelargonium* spp.). Other annuals are called "half-hardy" or weak perennials. These are plants capable of surviving the winter under the right conditions but not likely to do so and, therefore, are not reliable. Two garden favorites that are true perennials, though not very reliable, are dusty miller (*Senecio* spp.) and snapdragon (*Antirrhinum* spp.). Biennials ordinarily take two years to produce blossoms. However, some can bloom the first year from seed if they are started early indoors, or if sown in late summer or early fall. A garden favorite is the pansy (*Viola* spp.). Tropical perennials, weak perennials and some biennials are best treated as annuals. Grow them from seed, and discard them at the end of the growing season, to start with fresh seed and new young plants the following year. Annuals are great additions to the cutting garden as they are inexpensive, frequently easy to grow and respond well to cutting, providing blossoms for cutting from summer until frost.

Late summer provides the textures and colors of approaching autumn. An old bronze vase holds rich mahogany and brown sunflowers with apricot dahlias and creamy white roses. Zinnias and phlox contrast nicely with the larger flowers. Bells of Ireland, with their bright green, flowerlike bracts that loop over the edge of the container, provide textural interest.

These commercially grown snapdragons will soon be cut and sent to the flower markets. On a smaller scale, beautiful flowers such as these are easily grown and, when harvested, will provide long-lasting beauty and bright color in a vase or arrangement.

Biennials take two years to complete their life cycle. During the first year they grow vegetatively (leaves, roots and stems); they produce flowers the second season. At the end of the flowering period the biennial frequently sets seed and dies. Many biennials become permanent residents in the garden if a number of flowers are allowed to set seed and self-sow each year, allowing for continuation of the species and making impressive naturalized stands. The common foxglove (*Digitalis* spp.) is one of my favorite biennials.

Perennials are often overlooked in planning the cutting garden. Perennials live for two years or longer. Many perennials can come back year after year, and some will improve with age, producing more beautiful blooms with each passing year. Peonies (*Paeonia* spp.) and wormwood (*Artemisia* spp.) are two hardy perennials that improve with age, providing ever more materials for cutting as the years go by. Too frequently, perennials are linked with low-maintenance landscaping. Perennial plantings may save some aspects of garden maintenance, but don't think perennials are to be planted and left on their own. Like all plants, perennials respond best to good horticultural practices.

Woody plants are the ones that make up the permanent background of the garden. The trunks and branches form a lacy backdrop during the winter months and can provide shade and wind breaks, or form a pattern in the landscape that directs the eye; they can screen unpleasant views, too. Woody perennials are an excellent source of material for bouquets. The blossoms, of course, provide color, scent and texture; the foliage can fill a vase or help to cover the mechanics of an arrangement; and the bare twigs can add line and drama to an arrangement. Many trees and shrubs also provide fruit, a dramatic addition to a flower arrangement.

THE FORMAL CUTTING GARDEN

To some, a cutting garden means neat, orderly rows of flowers. To others it means long beds of flowers with verdant grassy strips dividing them. In some cases a separate area for cutting is fenced or hedged off from other garden features. The formal cutting garden can be any of these and more. I consider the formal cutting garden to be any garden in which the components are in place only for the production of cut flowers, and any aesthetic gain is of secondary value. In fact, a cutting garden can be downright ugly (though you may have to really work at making it so). The formal cutting garden is a utilitarian area that just happens to grow beauty.

The location of the cutting garden is important and will affect the success of your gardening venture and the variety of plants that can be grown. The best location for any cutting garden is in full sun, which benefits the widest variety of plants; although some cutting garden varieties might prefer partial shade, they can be satisfied by planting around trees, creating arbors and so forth. For the formal cutting garden a large rectangular area is ideal because it allows for the development of rows. There is no minimum or maximum size for a cutting garden; this is determined by the amount of land available and the quantity of flowers wanted. A 6-by-12-foot site planted largely with annuals is capable of producing enough blossoms and foliage to provide modest flower displays to decorate an average home. For gardeners with greater ambition, developing a larger garden will allow for greater diversity of cutting materials, larger bouquets and more of them. An extremely ambitious gardener may wish to expand the cutting garden to provide flowers for drying and including in everlasting bouquets, petals for potpourri and sachets and fresh blossoms for private use and gift giving. The scale of your site, your home and your needs will determine the type and size of cutting garden best for you.

Enclosing the cutting garden may be a wise step, for a number of reasons. Enclosure provides protection from animals; the white-tailed deer is our particular bane where I garden. Hedges, walls and fences all offer protection from damaging winds and can screen unsightly components of the landscape—yours or your neighbor's! (Such features as compost piles, utilitarian mulches and plant supports are essential to today's gardens but aren't the best-looking part of any landscape.) Formal or informal hedging is nice in larger gardens where there is enough room to ensure the hedge doesn't create problems with root and light compe-

tition. In smaller situations a fence or wall may be the more desirable alternative. Fences and walls may be used as plant supports for vining crops such as bittersweet, gourds, sweet peas, trumpet creeper and clematis.

The materials chosen to enclose a garden should be decided with consideration for the need and economics of the job. I have always fantasized about growing flowers within a brick wall, but as brick doesn't complement my home, landscape or checkbook, a wooden fence provides the landscape definition I seek. No matter what form of enclosure you may choose to employ, it is important to remember that you are raising flowers for cutting and that you don't want to hinder plant growth or your ability to work well in your garden. Plan adequate width for gates or other passways in and out of the garden so you can carry the necessary tools and equipment back and forth without skinning your knuckles.

The cutting garden should be handy. The landscape is more than just a bunch of pretty plants around a home; it should have purpose. Utilitarian areas such as vegetable gardens, herb gardens and cutting gardens should be located so that it is easy to run outdoors and pick a few blossoms before dinner or snip a rose to adorn your desk at work without making a major safari into the wilds of the landscape. An added benefit of keeping the cutting garden close to the home is that it is close to the center of all garden activities: water, tools, equipment and you!

The cutting garden at Mohonk Mountain House provides flowers for cutting and arranging fresh and some blooms for drying, for use in dried bouquets and potpourri. A mulch of wheat straw helps conserve moisture, keeps down weeds and provides a mud-free walkway for Mohonk florists.

A well-dressed cutting garden attractively fenced and softened with plantings. This handsomely designed cutting garden would be a delightful addition to any landscape. The paved path and wide gate provide easy access for florist and gardener alike.

Within the garden the planting rows or beds should run east to west. This allows all plants to benefit from maximum sun exposure. Arranging the shortest plants in the southernmost rows and the tallest plants as a backdrop on the northern edge will prevent taller plants from shading their neighbors.

Formal Cutting Garden Plan

PLANT LIST FOR A FORMAL CUTTING GARDEN (SUITABLE FOR USDA ZONE 5)

PERENNIALS AND HARDY BULBS

1. *Gypsophila paniculata* 'Bristol Fairy', baby's breath (1); underplant with *Allium giganteum* (8), 6 inches apart
2. *Miscanthus sinensis* (1)
3. *Delphinium elatum* 'Pacific Hybrids' (12), 12 inches apart
4. *Phlox paniculata*, garden phlox (9), 12 inches apart
5. *Astilbe* spp., assorted astilbe (7), 12 inches apart; underplant with mixed tulips (25)
6. *Heuchera sanguinea* 'Bressingham Hybrids', coral bells (3), 8 inches apart; underplant with mixed narcissuses (10)
7. *Aquilegia × hybrida* 'McKana Hybrids', columbine (5), 8 inches apart; underplant with mixed narcissuses (25)
8. *Digitalis purpurea*, foxglove (12), 6 inches apart
9. *Lilium ×* 'Connecticut Lemonglow', hybrid lily (12), 6 inches apart; underplant with *Myosotis sylvatica*, forget-me-nots
10. *Lilium ×* 'Sterling Star', hybrid lily (12), 6 inches apart; interplant with *Allium sphaerocephalum*, drumstick allium (16), 4 inches apart
11. *Rudbeckia hirta* 'Gloriosa Daisy' (6), 8 inches apart
12. *Helianthus annuus* 'Italian White', sunflower (5), 9 inches apart
13. *Lysimachia clethroides*, gooseneck lysimachia (12), 8 inches apart
14. *Achillea* 'Summer Pastels' (12), 6 inches apart
15. *Chrysanthemum maximum*, shasta daisy (12), 8 inches apart
16. *Rosa ×* 'Sunbright', hybrid tea rose (1); underplant with *Convallaria majalis*, lily of the valley (18)
17. *Lathyrus odoratus*, sweet pea (20), 6 inches apart; train to climb fencing
18. *Veronica spicata*, spike veronica (9), 4 inches apart
19. *Chrysanthemum × morifolium*, hardy garden chrysanthemum (8), 9 inches apart
20. *Hosta ×* 'Royal Standard' (3), 8 inches apart
21. *Lychnis coronaria* 'Angel Blush' (6), 6 inches apart
22. *Coreopsis grandiflora* 'Early Sunrise' (6), 6 inches apart
23. *Rosa ×* 'Garden Party', hybrid tea rose (1); underplant with *Viola tricolor*, Johnny-jump-ups
24. *Aconitum napellus*, monkshood (4), 9 inches apart
25. *Campanula persicifolia*, peach-leaved bellflower (8), 6 inches apart
26. *Monarda didyma*, bee balm, assorted colors (6), 12 inches apart
27. *Achillea ×* 'Coronation Gold' (8), 9 inches apart
28. *Liatris spicata*, gayfeather (24), 4 inches apart
29. *Paeonia lactiflora*, assorted peony (3), 18 inches apart
30. *Artemisia ludoviciana albula* 'Silver King' (5), 9 inches apart

ANNUALS AND TENDER BULBS

31. *Cleome hasslerana* 'Queen Mix', spider flower (6), 12 inches apart
32. *Cosmos bipinnatus* 'Sensation Mixed' (6), 12 inches apart
33. *Antirrhinum majus* 'Rocket Mixed', snapdragon (24), 6 inches apart
34. *Consolida orientalis* 'Imperial Mix', larkspur (24), 6 inches apart
35. *Zinnia elegans* 'State Fair Mix' (12), 9 inches apart
36. *Scabiosa atropurpurea* 'Imperial Mix', pincushion flower (18), 6 inches apart
37. *Celosia plumosa* 'Flamingo Feather' (6), 6 inches apart
38. *Amaranthus caudatus*, love-lies-bleeding (6), 8 inches apart
39. *Gladiolus*, assorted gladiola (12), 6 inches apart
40. *Zinnia elegans* 'Cut and Come Again' (9), 6 inches apart
41. *Ageratum houstonianum* 'Blue Horizon' (9), 6 inches apart
42. *Gomphrena globosa*, globe

amaranth (24), 6 inches apart
43. *Callistephus orientalis* 'Bouquet Mixed', aster (12), 8 inches apart
44. *Trachelium caeruleum*, purple umbrella (6), 6 inches apart
45. *Salvia farinacea* 'Blue Bedder' (6), 6 inches apart
46. *Tagetes signata* 'Lemon Gem,' signet marigold (9), 6 inches apart
47. *Xeranthemum annuum*, immortelle (6), 6 inches apart
48. *Acidanthera bicolor* (9), 4 inches apart

Allow enough space between rows or beds for ease in maintaining and harvesting the plants. Wider spacing may be a good idea on some rows to provide access for hoses, wheel barrows of compost and to permit you to pass through the garden without damaging plants.

An alternative to parallel rows or beds is a more formal and ornamental planting with geometrically arranged planting beds. This format is more reminiscent of a formal English or herb garden. The cutting garden diagrams at left and on page 15 show two designs, in the row and geometric styles. Each will produce enough material so vases of leftovers can be given away. When planting the formal cutting garden, it is best to place annuals in beds with annuals, and segregate perennials and biennials to their own area where they can't be disturbed by tilling or spading. The cutting garden is the perfect place for a nursery row. The nursery row is a space dedicated to growing or holding plants for later inclusion in the ornamental garden. Grow biennials such as *Campanula* from seed in the fall to transplant in the garden the following spring.

Carefully arranged to catch all the available sunlight and for easy maintenance, this cutting garden provides a wide variety of blooms from matricaria to cosmos and dahlias to salvia. The tall, fragrant Buddleia *is an inspired addition to the background of this hedged cutting garden.*

The curvilinear border of flowers softens the hedge in this landscape. Well-designed and-cared for, this border will provide loads of flowers and foliage for enjoying indoors in arrangements.

THE INTEGRATED GARDEN

Not everyone has the space for a garden with the sole purpose to provide cutting materials for indoor bouquets. For those of us with limited space, the integrated garden is a wonderful concept. Your space may demand plantings for screening, direction and aesthetics, but through careful plant selection and placement, you can have plenty of flowers for cutting incorporated into your shrubbery borders or flower beds. Even terrace and windowsill gardeners can incorporate a few flowers suitable for gracing a dining table or desktop.

The basis of integrated land-

scaping is to start with careful site analysis. Study the existing landscape and take note of those plants you currently grow and enjoy for cutting. Compare the plant lists provided in this book with herbaceous plants, shrubs, vines and trees that are already on site. Next, plan to enrich your existing landscape by selecting additional materials from the plant lists. Choose plants for your shady and sunny sites, adding trees, shrubs, spring-blooming bulbs, annuals and perennials to complete your landscape. To integrate your garden fully, find a niche for some culinary herbs,

Chosen with care, a few yellow tulips with a delicate rose blush provide warmth and complement the golden tones of an antique oak desk. The deep red bowl and the delicately blushed Amalanchier *buds provide contrasting texture and help to unify color.*

This old, glazed crock holds a rich array of summer colors. Even in tones of black, gray and white, though, the composition would be a study in textural contrasts: smooth against rough, fine against coarse.

The glory of autumn foliage and feathery plumes collected from the garden and byways.

some vegetables and some fruiting trees and shrubs. Not only will your landscape be beautiful but it will be useful as well, a pleasure for all the senses.

This book isn't meant to be a tutorial on landscape design, but I will occasionally use this space to introduce some of the design elements useful for both the landscape and the vase. Perhaps the most important element of design is function. The landscape must serve a need: to improve or hide a view; to direct the eye or garden visitor; or to provide a harvest of flowers, vegetables or herbs. Flowers arranged in a vase also have function: to decorate a dining table, to accentuate a specific architectural feature or to cover an unsightly flaw; the form the flowers will take in the vase is determined by the function of that arrangement.

Other facets of design are scale, or proportion. Scale is a function of size relationships. The larger the space, the larger the plants can be to fill that space. When dealing with flowers in vases, scale is easily understood. Large flowers placed in tiny vases look silly and give the impression of being top heavy. A tiny vase of flowers centered in the middle of a large dining table looks insignificant and is dwarfed by the expanse of its surroundings.

Texture in the visual sense is the appearance of materials, whether in the landscape or in a vase. Playing a variety of textures off each other heightens the visual excitement of the composition. I liken this to rubbing first sandpaper and

then velvet; the velvet feels all the softer after the fingers have experienced coarse sandpaper. In the garden try combining astilbe and hosta, for example. The soft, feathery plumes of astilbe seem to appear even more fluffy when viewed next to the smooth texture of the large hosta leaves.

Perhaps the design element that receives the most attention is color. Color can seem cool, as in the case of blue, lavender and green, or hot, as in the case of orange, red and bright pink. Combinations of color can be subtle, bold, monochromatic or multicolored. Careful use of color in the landscape can create interest, attract attention to specific areas, make portions of the garden seem to recede in the landscape or magically bring the farthest corner of the garden closer. Dark colors recede in a shady nook, for example, whereas bright colors such as yellow and white bring the farthest corners closer. Color preference is a personal matter. We all have favorite colors that appear in our home decor or our wardrobe. Color in the integrated cutting garden will reappear in the home when flowers are harvested and brought indoors.

Rhythm as it applies to design always reminds me of the old roadside Burma Shave signs of a generation ago. They were situated to flow in sequence at a natural pace as one drove along. In the garden or vase, of course, rhythm isn't a matter of spacing a few signs. Rather, it is placing elements in a natural way so the eye can

appreciate them without interruption in its natural flow. Some guidelines for rhythm will be helpful to the novice designer. An odd number of elements is invariably more successful than an even number. I don't actually count numbers of flowers when I start to arrange, and one can make dynamite arrangements using even numbers of flowers, but threes, fives and sevens tend to create a natural rhythm without forming stiff, easily recognized lines or boxes. Unlike some commercially grown flowers, garden flowers grow in a variety of sizes and shapes; even blossoms cut from the same plant may be of different sizes. When trying to achieve balance, proportion and rhythm in an arrangement, it is a good idea to place the smaller, individual flowers toward the outside. This means the higher an element is placed in an arrangement, the smaller it should be.

Rhythm in the garden is affected by plant placement. Remember, when placing plants in the landscape, smaller plants musn't be shaded by larger plants. Short plants deserve a place in the foreground of the border, whereas larger specimens will be more appreciated at the back of the border where they won't cover their more diminutive neighbors.

The best effect is gained by planting in multiples, and when the plants mature they will appear as a single grouping. This is as true of many trees and shrubs as it is of annuals and perennials. Planting multiples will prevent a busy look, and

PLANT LIST FOR AN INTEGRATED CUTTING GARDEN (SUITABLE FOR USDA ZONE 5)

WOODY PLANTS

1. *Malus* spp., crabapple (1)
2. *Oxydendron arborescens,* sorrel tree (1)
3. *Tsuga canadensis,* Canadian hemlock (1)
4. *Thuja occidentalis,* arborvitae (1)
5. *Deutzia gracillis,* slender deutzia (3)
6. *Kalmia latifolia,* mountain laurel (1)
7. *Rosa* spp., climbing rose (1)
8. *Rhododendron* spp., azalea (2)

HERBACEOUS PLANTS

9. *Hosta* × 'Royal Standard', perennial (24); underplant with daffodils and narcissuses (48)
10. *Hosta* × 'So Sweet', perennial (24)
11. *Convallaria majus,* lily of the valley, perennial (36)
12. *Nicotiana alata* 'Fragrant Cloud', annual (12); allow to self-sow
13. *Miscanthus sinensis* 'Zebrinus', perennial (1)

14. *Delphinium elatum* 'Pacific Hybrids', perennial (8)
15. *Digitalis purpurea,* foxglove, biennial (12); allow to self-sow
16. *Paeonia lactifolia,* peony, perennial (6)
17. *Gypsophila paniculata* 'Bristol Fairy', baby's breath, perennial (1); underplant with giant alliums (8)
18. *Achillea* × 'Coronation Gold', yarrow, perennial (6)
19. *Artemisia ludoviciana albula* 'Silver King', perennial (5)
20. *Aquilegia* × *hybrida* 'McKana Hybrids', columbine, perennial (6)
21. *Cosmos bipinnatus* 'Sensation Mixed', annual (12)
22. *Zinnia elegans* 'Cut and Come Again', annual (12); underplant with mixed tulips (24)
23. *Antirrhinum majus* 'Rocket Mixed', snapdragon, annual (36); underplant with tulips (36)
24. *Molucella laevis,* bells of Ireland, annual (6)
25. *Tagetes signata* 'Lemon Gem', signet marigold, annual (18); underplant with tulips (24)

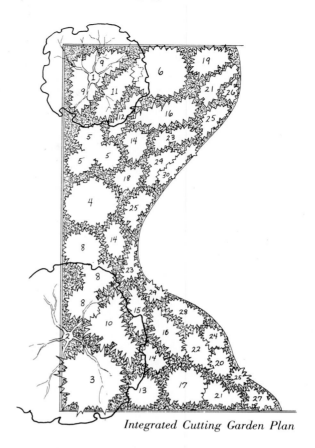

Integrated Cutting Garden Plan

26. *Reseda odorata,* mignonette, annual (12)
27. *Amaranthus caudatus,* lovelies-bleeding, annual (6)
28. *Callistephus chinensis* 'Powder Puff Bouquet', aster, annual (8)
29. *Scabiosa atropurpurea* 'Imperial Mixed', pincushion flower, annual (12)
30. *Tropaeolum majus* 'Glorious Glean', nasturtium, annual (12)

help bring the garden picture together. Repeating clusters of certain plants, colors, textures or lines will create rhythm and add to the unified effect.

The integrated cutting garden shown in the plan above is designed to be both beautiful in the landscape and provide a generous source of materials for cutting. This garden plan considers the elements of design: color, texture, line, function, scale and rhythm. Notice the intentional creation of shade using small trees suitable for cutting and year-'round interest in the landscape, and the selection of plants with seasonal fruits, berries or pods and interesting bark or twig configuration. When harvesting materials from the integrated cutting garden, remember that the integrated garden has several functions. You may harvest several stems of peony blooms, but you must remember this will detract slightly from the overall landscape effect. With this in mind, plant enough of each variety for both cutting and landscape display.

THE CUTTING GARDEN PLANTING AND GROWING GUIDE

No matter what style of garden you have the time, energy and land to support, success in the cutting garden relies on plant selection, site preparation and planting. Take the time to do the job right in the beginning, and the payback will be healthier plants with greater production of cutable flowers and larger and more perfect blooms. Choose the right plant for the site. This is a basic axiom of good horticulture. Trying to grow plants under less-than-favorable conditions will invariably be an invitation to trouble. Plants grown in inadequate light will be leggy as they stretch to reach the sun. Flower stems may be weak and production will be diminished. When planning for an area not in full sun, choose plants that do well in shade or dappled sunlight such as astilbe, hosta and nicotiana (see "Flowers for the Shady Cutting Garden," page 88). Similarly, don't expect hosta or other shade lovers to thrive in full sun.

Take the time to become acquainted with your garden. Some areas offer light shade but will support such plants as snapdragons, which thrive in full sun and require cool conditions. Drainage patterns and soil types can affect the success of your garden ventures.

If bread is the staff of life for the body, then soil is the staff of life for the garden. All plants require water, nutrients and air to grow, and these are supplied by the soil. Most of us garden in less-than-desirable soils. Sometimes we joke that our gardens yield more rock than soil, or that we might just as well be growing plants at the beach. The best soil for the greatest variety of plants is a rich, well-draining garden loam. *Loam* describes soil texture; typically it is an equal mix of sand, silt and clay particles. A loam soil will hold its shape (remember dirt bombs?) when compressed in a fist into a ball but will not show the details of the hand print. Heavier or more claylike soils will also form a ball when compressed, but on close inspection, you will be able to identify details of the hand print (the ultimate dirt bomb). Clay soils tend to drain poorly and can become very hard—like concrete, if not carefully handled. Sandy soils will not easily form a ball when compressed and collapse when the fist is relaxed. Sandy soils usually drain too well and offer plants poor nutrition, as water moves quickly through the sand, carrying the nutrients away into the subsoil. Most of us garden on some mixture of the three soil types, and any garden soil, somewhere be-

A cutting garden, planted in the wide-row style. Asters, bachelor buttons, signet marigolds, cirsium and pansies provide abundant flowers for bouquets.

Clay soil compressed in the hand will form a dense "dirt bomb," showing details of the handprint.

Sandy soil compressed in the hand will not hold together and crumbles easily when pressure is released.

Loamy soil will form a loose "dirt bomb" when compressed, but will not show the details of the handprint, and will crumble easily.

tween pure sand and pure clay, offers good garden potential.

If your soil is less than adequate, what can you do? The answer to most soil problems is organic matter in any of a number of forms: compost, leaf mold, peat moss, well-rotted manure or green manure crops. (Green manure refers to particular plants that are seeded, grown briefly and then turned into the soil, where the tender young shoots quickly break down and become part of the organic portion of the soil.) Organic matter added to any soil benefits that soil. The bulk of organic matter will lighten a heavy or claylike soil, increasing the space between soil particles and allowing for faster drainage and more air around the roots to stimulate root growth. In addition, organic matter helps bind tiny soil particles together into aggregate particles. In a sandy soil, organic matter will help increase water-holding capacity and hold some nutrients that are easily washed away by water traveling through the soil. I liken organic matter to fiber in the human diet; it's essential to keep everything working as it should. It isn't enough to have one dose of dietary fiber during a lifetime, it is likewise essential to add organic matter to the garden continuously to keep soil happy and healthy.

Prepare the site for your cutting garden well in advance of planting time. Outline your beds and determine the location of rows and borders. Begin incorporating organic matter in as many forms as possible—it is difficult to overindulge your

soil in organic matter. Adding a total of 4 to 6 inches of organic matter is a good start. Mix the soil well. For woody plants or long-lived perennials, this is your one opportunity to enrich the soil thoroughly.

Have the pH of your soil tested. PH is the measure of acidity/alkalinity. Tests for pH are simple and often done at no cost at local cooperative extension headquarters and even some garden centers. Is it necessary to add topsoil to your existing soil? *Topsoil* is a term frequently misused. People generally envision topsoil as a wonderfully dark, rich loam soil ideal for plant growth. Unfortunately, there are no regulations for topsoil, and the quality varies greatly with the purveyor and source. In fact, buying topsoil can sometimes do more harm than good. Buy topsoil only if you need to change the grade of your property. Examine the soil before delivery and make sure it doesn't come from land treated with herbicides.

When you are ready to prepare the soil, choose a day when it is moist but not soggy. If you can hear squishing as you walk or can squeeze water from a handful of soil, or if soil clings overmuch to tools or shoes, it is probably too wet to work without destroying soil texture. Wet soils tend to lose structure when worked or when they receive too much foot or vehicular traffic. It is a good idea to perform other garden duties when soils are wet. If soils are too dry and powdery, it is a good idea to wait until after a rain, or water the site a

day or two before working the soil, so that it will have a nice, moist texture.

Some of the best gardens are double dug. Double digging is a method by which you loosen and enrich the soil to a depth of 16 to 18 inches. Double digging benefits the garden for years to come. After the initial garden preparation, add the soil amendments. These can be mixed into the soil using the more traditional garden turning method or with a rotary tiller. I love to work with soil and find the creation of rich, well-prepared soil a warming, fulfilling experience. There is nothing more satisfying than a well-prepared planting bed.

If you have done your soil preparation in advance of planting, perhaps in the fall before a spring planting, I recommend the use of a cover crop such as winter rye or winter wheat that will grow over the winter and then be turned under in the spring. This will hold the soil in place and discourage weeds. For areas of a few square feet, it may be more practical to mulch this area well with shredded leaves, compost, straw or pine needles to protect the soil from exposure to washing rains and blowing wind. Nature almost never leaves bare soil unprotected.

When it comes to planting, always choose plants that can be expected to do well in your environment; don't impose your environment on plants that won't be happy there. Plants purchased for inclusion in your cutting garden should come from a reputable dealer. Choose varieties with care, as some breeders have worked to develop varieties that are short and may not be good for cutting. The plant portraits (page 45) recommend specific varieties to ask for. Look for plants that are strong and actively growing in the spring. Yellowed foliage or faded flowers in the pot or the plant pack suggest they have been neglected, exposed to extreme conditions or should have been transplanted already.

Dig a hole a little larger than the root system of each plant to be sure the roots are not crowded. Leave enough room so that the plant can mature without crowding its neighbors. The mature spacing depends on the plant, but generally speaking, tall plants need more space than the more petite ones. Carefully remove the plant from its container (plants slip out of their pots or cells much more readily when wet). On very root-bound specimens

it is always a good idea to slice through the root system in two or three locations from the top of the root ball to the bottom to encourage new roots to branch out into the soil.

Place the plants in the garden at the same depth they were at in the pots or cells. Firm the soil around the base of the plant, and water in well with a watering can or breaker (see Watering in the Garden, page 21) to settle the soil around the root ball. Until young plants are thoroughly established in their new location it may be necessary to water frequently so that plants will not be stressed as they develop new supporting root systems.

Note: Plants benefit from a second application of fertilizer in midseason. This "side-dress" fertilizer dosage is applied in a band around each plant. Avoid direct contact between plant stems and fertilizer, as the fertilizer may burn.

Double digging is the best way to prepare flower beds for planting.

WIDE-ROW PLANTING IN THE CUTTING GARDEN

In the cutting garden, wide-row plantings are more practical than single rows. A row of plants one plant wide (single row) requires more space for the "aisles" between rows; the plants are more exposed to wind and compacted soils. Wide rows may be from 18 to 36 inches wide and as long as the garden. Each row is basically a bed of plants. Plants grown in wide rows are surrounded by other plants, not by the hard, compacted soil of walkways. Plants grown side by

side in wide rows will shade out weeds that compete for nutrients and water. Each plant is supported by its neighbors. This way you have less staking to do and can frequently provide plant support for a whole

Well-prepared soil is healthy soil, and healthy soil yields healthy plants. The lush growth and heavy bloom on this Brugmansia (angel's trumpet) in the Mohonk Gardens is an indication of a well-tended garden soil. Copious amounts of organic matter added each year ensure good results.

Asters for cutting have long, straight stems and are borne on tall plants. Many dwarf strains of aster are sold for bedding as well. Be sure the varieties you choose for inclusion in your cutting garden will produce cutting stems.

Plants staked for protection from summer rains and winds are grown in a cutting garden at Mohonk Mountain House. The sturdy bamboo stakes are placed next to plants at the beginning of the growing season.

block of plants rather than individuals. Perhaps the biggest advantage to wide-row planting is the space savings. Space is at a premium in any garden. A garden located near a water source in full sun, and soil that has been enriched and is ready for planting are valuable commodities. Use those enriched soil areas as growing spaces, not for paths between rows of plants.

For wide-row plantings some support may be necessary, but the single-stake method may not be suitable. Corner supports can hold weave-wire fencing horizontally about 1 foot over the row. Plants can grow through the wire and get the support they need. Another useful method of supporting plants grown in rows is to provide sturdy support at each end of the row and stretch tiers of heavy twine or wire along the length of the row, trellis style. Plants can be secured to the wire or allowed to lean against the trellis.

In the integrated cutting garden, support should be more discrete. Many plant supports are sold in garden shops and from mail-order houses. They provide a neat, finished look when incorporated in the garden, and are frequently designed to last for many seasons. For generations, European gardeners have used twiggy branches of shrubs or trees to stake plants in the garden. Choose a branch of suitable height and firmly implant it in the ground at the base of the young plants (but not so near as to damage their roots). As the plants grow up through the twigs, they gain support without being "tied to the stake" and cover the branch at the same time. If using bamboo, choose stakes dyed green as they will blend discretely with foliage.

No matter what staking method you choose, it should support the plant throughout the season. Be careful to tie plants to supports with twine or covered-wire twisters that won't cut into tender stems. Some gardeners use strips of cloth. Allow a generous space between stake, stem and plant tie to avoid cutting into and girdling tender stems. Girdled stems are less efficient and result in stunted plant growth, or may kill the plant outright. Improper plant support can damage stems, weakening them and making them more prone to breakage. Nothing is more frustrating than nurturing a plant to the brink of flower production only to have it damaged as a result of poor staking or no staking!

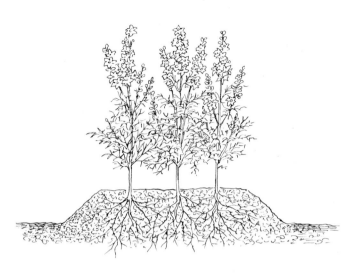

Wide-row planting, as with this planting of larkspur, creates orderly plant communities. Among the benefits are root support and decreased weed growth.

PEST CONTROL

Pest control in the garden begins in the planning stage. Pests in the garden are a nuisance, but never is an aphid infestation or botrytis outbreak more disheartening than when you find it has made flowers that appear passable in the garden unsuitable for harvesting and using indoors in arrangements. The sight of a string of aphids marching boldly across the dining table in search of new marigolds to explore is beyond compare. A pest control program need not be expensive, time-consuming or injurious to the environment. Success in controlling pests is nothing more than good garden practices.

When it comes to winning the battle against pests, careful attention to site selection and bed preparation are critical to success. Choose plants that will perform well in your garden, for they will be best equipped to fend off attacks by pests and disease. Every garden has microclimates that offer nuances of sunlight, heat, drainage and so forth. Learn about the microclimates in your garden and use them to maximize your cutting garden's growing capacity.

Carefully study the varieties available from your favorite seed source or garden center, and choose those varieties that offer disease resistance or tolerance. Inbred disease resistance isn't a feature of every variety, but it is a necessity for some plants—asters, for example. The key words are *resistance* and *tolerance*. These mean exactly what they say. A plant resistant to a disease will be less likely to get the disease; still, when that plant's resistance is weakened by poor growing conditions or constant bombardment with disease spores, the inbred resistance

Watering in the Garden

In the garden, water ensures good plant growth and is essential for new plants to establish themselves. All too frequently I see people spraying their plants with hoses and the kind of nozzles designed for washing cars. Delicate misty sprays are great for young seedlings, but more mature plants need larger amounts of water aimed at the roots. Invest in an old-fashioned watering can, good for watering a few plants, and a breaker with an extension handle for supplying a generous amount of water around the plants' roots. Water breakers look very much like shower heads and behave in the same way, dividing a steady stream of water into numerous, more gentle streams. The quantity of water is not altered, but the force is "broken" and the effectiveness is improved.

Wide-row planting provides beds 24 inches wide with 18-inch rows between. Mulched paths reduce soil compaction and improve water conservation and weed reduction. The plants in the rows are planted four or five across. They help support each other and create a dense canopy that further inhibits weed growth.

may become ineffective. *Tolerance* is a term that means that a plant may "carry" the disease without showing symptoms or effect. Diseases may become symptomatic even on tolerant plants, if they are weakened by poor growing conditions.

Once plants have been selected, don't skimp on planting or care. A wise gardener once told me that you should dig a $10 hole for a $2 plant; in other words, take the time to plant your living investment well. Seeds, seedlings, nursery-grown perennials and woody plants all need some nursing and special care during the first weeks of life in your garden. The first few days or weeks are critical. Remember, water is the important element during this time. Like humans, plants can live for a long time without "food," but life is snuffed out remarkably quickly without water. The key to successful pest control is to keep plants healthy and stress free. Healthy growth requires adequate nutrition.

So, you've done everything right and still have insect and disease problems. Time to go to the sprayer and chemical arsenal, right? Wrong! Keep trying to maintain plant vigor and health through good gardening practices such as proper watering and fertility. Don't neglect weeding! I've always looked on weeding as a great mind release—my own style of meditation. Weeds crowd plants and can encourage diseases by stifling air flow around them; stagnant, damp air can encourage disease. Weeds are also great competitors for water and nutrients. Use mulches to control weeds and help maintain constant soil moisture levels.

Good gardening means going into the garden with eyes wide open and on the look-out for discolored leaves, the first Japanese beetle or a wilting seedling. Often these are the first indications of trouble brewing. What to do when you see that first beetle? Kill it—that's right, kill it! Just pick it up and squish it. It's as simple as that.

In the amount of time it takes to apply a pesticide, you can hand-pick and destroy all sorts of pests before they have a chance to multiply and populate your entire garden. Diseased leaves can also be picked, a good means of control if symptoms are noticed early. Once a disease has spread, you may do more damage than good if you hand-pick diseased leaves to the point of defoliating plants. If only one plant of many shows symptoms, consider roguing the entire plant. If leaves are falling off the plant due to disease, gather them and remove them from the garden. Don't add these harbingers of disease to your compost heap; you will just invite trouble later on. Insects that are too small to hand-pick are sometimes easy to spray off with the water hose. Hand-picking, bug squishing and aphid washing are all examples of cultural controls. Repeat cultural controls as necessary. Cultural controls were the mainstay of garden pest control

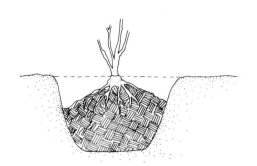  

When planting nursery-grown plants, always create a hole larger than the existing root ball. Arrange the soil depth so that the plant will be at the same depth as it was in the nursery. Then backfill with soil that has been amended with organic matter. Tamp the soil carefully to eliminate air pockets before watering in well.

programs before the days of chemical pesticides, the inaccurately named "wonder drugs" of the plant world.

If all else fails, and sometimes it does, it may become necessary to introduce a pesticide into the landscape to control an insect or disease. Pesticides need not be dangerous chemicals. A few drops of liquid detergent in water has some insecticidal action. With environmental concerns in mind, pesticide manufacturers are looking for products that do the job of eliminating unwanted populations with minimal hazard to the environment and user. Many new products are biological or botanical pesticides. Your local cooperative extension agent can advise you as to which products are safest to use.

As the gardening season draws to a close, the garden still needs attention. Annuals in the cutting garden are often still going strong until hit by frost. A killing frost will damage the tender annuals first, leaving some such as snapdragons to continue producing until late in the season. Some plants such as *Echinacea*, *Rudbeckia*, *Nigella* and *Scabiosa* provide interesting seed heads for dried arrangements. Healthy annuals damaged by frost can be added to compost heaps where they will break down and provide lots of valuable organic matter.

Carefully lift and store tender roots for next year. Dig the tubers of the most successful dahlias, favorite gladiolas and *Acidanthera*. Clean off excess garden soil and remove damaged roots. Allow them to dry for several days in a shaded, frost-free location. Pack in slightly damp sand, peat moss or wood shavings and store in a cool, frost-free place until spring. Be sure to examine these roots at every step of the overwintering process for signs of insects or disease, and discard any that show signs of infestation.

Labels are critical, as memory often fades with the bright autumn foliage. Be as explicit as possible. Although names are important, you'll save time if you also provide your own description: "My favorite apricot dahlia, three feet tall, best cutting stems!" Organize labels, stakes and pots, not only to protect them from winter weather but to give you a head start in spring. Make notes in a notebook. Your end-of-season notes will reward you ten-fold next spring.

The first killing frost marks the official end of the gardening season—or does it? The autumn garden is full of cutting opportunities. Brightening fall foliage deserves a place indoors. Fall-blooming asters and chrysanthemums last for weeks and look refreshed when arranged with bright scarlet and yellow leaves. The cutting garden continues to yield berries, interesting twig shapes and bark textures as well as dried flowers and seedpods until the snow flies.

The approach of winter indicates the need for protection for tender plantings, exposed broad-leaved evergreen shrubs and newly planted perennials and bulbs. Winter protection may consist of snow fencing; burlap wind breaks; or branches of pine, spruce or fir placed against tender evergreen shrubs. Pine straw, evergreen boughs and straw also provide good insulating cover for bulbs and tender and evergreen perennials. Snow is the best insulating cover, but in areas where snow cover may be suspect, 3 to 6 inches of lightweight mulch will do the job. The concept of winter mulch is not to keep the soil warm. Applied after the ground has started to freeze, a winter mulch will help keep the soil uniformly frozen, and then will help prevent damage from frost heaving due to freezing, thawing and refreezing of soils.

When preparing garden plants for winter, avoid tightly wrapping plants, especially with clear or dark plastics. Light-colored, "breathable" fabrics may be used to protect, but in wrapping plants tightly, you run the risk of heat buildup on sunny days that may cause winter buds to break dormancy or encourage an outbreak of fungal organisms.

Maintaining healthy plants in the garden is a combination of proper cultural techniques and good plant selection. Matricaria (fever few), Artemisia and Nepeta (cat mint) are usually free from insects and disease when grown under ideal circumstances.

HARVESTING THE CUTTING GARDEN

Harvesting flowers and greens from the cutting garden is wonderfully rewarding. Picking flowers is a pastime we enjoy from childhood. The term *picking* brings to mind small, pudgy, childish fingers grasping delicate flower stems and wrestling tattered blossoms from the parent plants to be presented in a woeful, endearing bouquet.

Cutting flowers from the home garden has an advantage to using the commercial florist; we have the ability to choose specific blooms with the size and shape we need. Always look for flowers that are still maturing and developing, and free of insects and disease. Flowers that are starting to fade should be harvested and discarded before the plant sets seed, as you would in deadheading any garden. Older flowers will not last as long in a bouquet as younger blooms. An occasional damaged petal may be carefully removed from most flowers without altering the overall beauty of the blossom.

Success in harvesting flowers depends on three factors: sharp cuts, clean water and containers, and proper pruning or cutting. Let's look at the act of cutting flowers. Flowers are attached to the plants with stems. Sometimes individual flowers are attached closely together along the stem, as in snapdragons. In other instances, single blossoms may be found at the end of a stem, as in asters. If you consider harvesting stems instead of blossoms, the harvesting of flowers is basically the same. An understanding of the basics of pruning and plant structure will help you get the most from each cut in the garden. With most plants, both vegetative (leaves and stems) and reproductive (flowers) growth starts out as buds. Buds are found along the stems of plants, and usually it is easy to tell vegetative buds from flower buds. Flower buds are plump and rounded. Vegetative

Cutting stems of flowers is an act of pruning. Care should be taken to balance stem length with foliage loss which will affect plant health.

Mohonk Flower Girl, circa 1901. Courtesy of the Mohonk Mountain House Archives.
Gathering flowers for a bouquet from the garden is still a rewarding experience today.

The Knife Myth

Almost every flower-arranging book I have read over the years states unequivocally that you must make cuts with a sharp knife. Few of them actually tell you how it is done without damaging plants and drawing blood from straining fingers. Many professional florists do use a knife as they find it less cumbersome to use. By grasping the knife handle between the pad of the thumb and the ring and pinkie fingers, you can work with thumb, first and middle fingers to handle flowers. The technique is to hold the knife stationary in the hand and hold the flower stem at an angle between knife and thumb. Hold the flower stem in the left hand and pull the knife back with the right hand while holding it tightly against the stem. The blade will cut the stem and not move against the thumb. This technique takes time to perfect and works best with a relatively short, straight-bladed knife. Your knife, like other tools, must be kept clean and sharp. A dull knife will make you work harder and strain with the blade, and it is when you are straining that the knife may slip and cause injury.

There is no reason why you can't achieve excellent results when using good, clean, sharp pruning tools. If the cut is clean and the tool is clean, the stem will function well in a vase of water.

buds are frequently found in the axils of leaves where leaves join stems. When cutting, if you make a sharp cut back to a vegetative bud you will encourage a new stem from that bud. All cuts should be made with a clean pruner or utility shears. Cut close to the bud, leaving about ¼ inch above the bud. Whether cutting flowers or pruning, you can control the shape of the plant and the direction of new growth by cutting to buds that face away from the center of the plant. Outward-facing buds will produce new stem growth in the direction they are facing. By pruning this way, you encourage new growth that will receive maximum sun and allow for open branching, which is less prone to disease.

Some plants don't produce lateral buds and will not branch when cut, among them many of the bulbous plants such as tulips, lilies and gladioluses. Bulbous plants need to produce as much foliage as possible to maintain bulb health and vigor. When harvesting tulips and their like, take only as much stem length as necessary for your design. Leave as much foliage as possible to strengthen the bulb. To

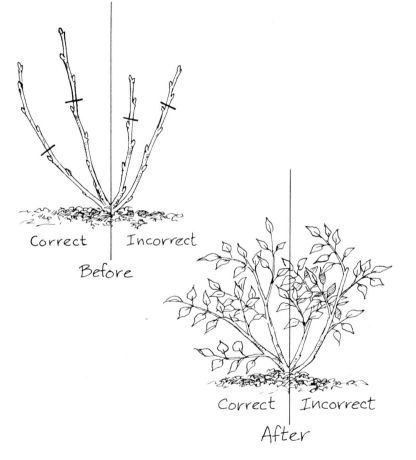

Correct | Incorrect

Before

Correct | Incorrect

After

When used properly, a sharp knife will cut the stem and not the hand!

Harvesting flower stems from woody plants not only affects the shape of the plant, but will affect its health, as well. Carefully make cuts that will "open up" the center of the plant and eliminate problems in the future.

maximize stem length, professional cut-flower growers will uproot an entire plant and cut off the bulb at the base of the stem. You may choose to take this extreme measure with some plants, but be forewarned the bulb will probably never produce again.

Trees and shrubs offer many wonderful cut flowers, fresh greens and attractive, seasonal fruits. Forcing flowers in the winter months is greatly rewarding and easy to do (see page 33). Winter cutting should only be done when air temperatures are above freezing. Be very careful when cutting from woody plants because the woody structure is permanent. The basic pruning rules still apply. When cutting from trees and shrubs, cut stems flush with a branch or cut back to an outward-facing bud or budded branch.

A wide variety of cutting tools is available from mail-order catalogs, garden centers, nurseries and hardware stores. The tool should be clean and sharp. I prefer lightweight utility shears for work with most herbaceous materials. When you have to strain to use the lightweight shears, it means the tool can't handle the job. Trying to cut too heavy a stem with lightweight tools may damage the shears, the stem or both. Ragged cuts on the stem will have a more difficult time absorbing water. Ragged cuts left on the plant invite disease and insect infestations. For heavy or woody stems up to ½ inch in diameter, a hand pruner is the tool of choice. I recommend a shear-type pruner (my favorite has replaceable parts, including springs and blades). When stems exceed ½ inch it may be necessary to bring out the lopping shears. Lightweight loppers appear to have the blade mechanism of the hand pruner with extended handles to increase leverage. Not only do loppers increase cutting potential but they provide added reach, handy when working with large shrubs or small trees.

You may want a flowering or fruiting branch that is clearly out of reach. Though ladders are an option, they are unstable in most garden situations. A pole pruner with an extension handle will provide cutting ability at heights of 10 or more feet. Choose the right tool for the job. The investment in a few extra moments to go and get the lopper will save time, strain, extend the life of your hand pruner and give you the quality cut needed to extend the life of the cut stem and ensure continued health of the tree or shrub in the garden.

Woody stems of mountain laurel and Polygonum *require time to condition. For best results, pick flowers in the evening the day before they are to be used, and condition them overnight in a cool location.*

WHEN TO HARVEST

With care, flowers can be successfully harvested at any time of the day. For the most successful arrangements, I recommend that you cut in the cool of the evening and let your fresh-cut flowers condition in water in a cool place overnight. Experience and a hectic lifestyle prove, however, that we don't always have the time to harvest under ideal conditions. We must "cut when the knife is sharp," to quote my mentor, Ruth Smiley, guardian angel of the Mohonk Mountain House Gardens for more than 50 years. And so we find ourselves picking flowers under the noonday sun and by flashlight or in the rain. As the seasons change, the ideal picking time varies somewhat. As August passes to September it is good to pick during the warmer afternoon hours when the plants have started to draw water from their roots. Plants that thrive in hot weather really appreciate the midafternoon heat.

CONDITIONING

Many flowers are happy to go from garden to vase and will last very nicely without special treatment. However, I've found that the life expectancy of cut flowers and greens will greatly increase when cut flowers and greens are "conditioned" before finding a home in a vase of water. This is even more important when designing flowers in floral foam such as Oasis or when using devises such as pin holders or marbles. During the conditioning process, flowers and greens absorb water unimpeded until all the plant parts are completely pumped with water and turgid.

When flowers are cut in the garden they are not quite ready to plunge into water. Careful preparation of cut materials is another step. After coming in

Artemisia *and* Xeranthemum *dry easily when suspended upside down in a warm, dry, dark place.*

Large-petaled daisy flowers such as Rudbeckia *can be difficult to condition successfully. For successful arrangements, take the time to condition them properly.*

Temperature Requirements of Common Garden Cut Flowers and Foliage

Cool (room) temperatures are best for spring-flowering herbaceous plants such as violets, forget-me-nots, spring-flowering bulbs such as tulips and the tender foliage of ferns.

Warm temperatures (100 to 120 degrees Fahrenheit) will condition the widest variety of flowers and foliage. When conditioning an unfamiliar species, try warm water first; chances are it will give excellent results.

Hot water (about 150 degrees Fahrenheit) is best for cuttings from trees and shrubs. On tender plants hot water may actually cause tender stems to break down and impede their success. Hot water is best for roses, hydrangea, lilacs, crab-apples and flowering cherries.

Consult the plant portraits (page 45) for the recommended conditioning temperatures for plants included in this book.

from the garden, take the time to remove carefully most of the foliage from each flower stem. The more foliage is removed, the better the blossom will last in the vase. It is essential to remove any foliage that will be under water during the conditioning process and later in the vase. With some plants it is effective to grasp the stem loosely above the set of leaves you wish to remove and pull downward toward the base of the stem. Tools sold as stem "strippers" will also do the job, but I feel that most of them do unnecessary damage to tender stems. Discard healthy foliage into a basket for incorporation in the compost heap. The occasional stem may resist stripping and you may find it necessary to use a knife or snips to remove foliage. Now is the time to remove thorns that may interfere with handling later on. Thorns and stubs left on the stems may cause difficulty during arranging as they tend to grasp other stems and make moving them in the vase more difficult.

When foliage and thorns have been removed, recut the stems at an angle, making sure the cut is clean with no ragged edges, and plunge the stems in clean, fresh water up to the lowest set of leaves. Almost any container may be used to condition flowers as long as it is clean and will hold water. If you are a recycler, be wary of containers that formerly held household cleaning products; the residue may be toxic. Cleanliness cannot be stressed enough! Between each use and the next, take the time to clean the container thoroughly. Dirt is the death knell of cut flowers and greens. Residue left in conditioning buckets and in vases breed bacteria, and bacteria clog the cut stems of flowers and foliage, reducing water uptake. Use a disinfectant solution such as chlorine bleach to clean and disinfect containers between each use.

Woody plants are handled in a different fashion. The foliage is stripped as for other cuts; be sure to do a thorough job of it. Some flowering shrubs such as lilacs do best when all the leaves have been removed and so the water absorbed by the stem goes only to the flower. After you have stripped off foliage, make two 1-inch-long cuts into the cut end of the stem using a proper or snips. These cuts should be made along the length of the stem and in effect will quarter the stem. This will increase the woody stem's ability to take up water. Some sources have recommended using a hammer to crush the stems to increase water absorption. I have always felt that the crushed stems will be less able to draw water and are sites that will be susceptible to bacterial growth.

One school of thought insists on cutting all stems under water to prevent exposure to air, which may enter and move up the stem, blocking the passage of water. The logistical challenge of accomplishing this feat when handling a lot of flowers and foliage is daunting. In my experience, success is achievable without cutting stems under water or using specially designed cutters that do the job for you. Properly prepared stems that have been conditioned will be just fine without being cut under water, as long as the cutting tool is sharp and the water and container are clean.

Water temperature is another critical factor in successful conditioning. Most plants prefer one of three water temperature categories: cool water (room temperature), warm or tepid (100 to 120 degrees Fahrenheit) and hot water (about 150 degrees Fahrenheit). Some plants, especially woody plants, require water that is almost boiling to condition or rescue them. When bringing in difficult woody plants such as mock orange (or sometimes even roses), place them in about ½ inch of boiling hot water (don't attempt to keep the water boiling). When the water cools to warm, place the prepared stems into a deep container of hot water and condition overnight. During the conditioning process, containers of prepared flowers are best stored in a cool place away from the sun. Allow the water temperature to cool naturally and in the morning the flowers will be fully turgid and ready for designing.

Several agents to add to the conditioning or vase water have been suggested over the years. Some are based on fact, others on speculation or myth. "Flower food" or floral preservative is sold in flower shops and garden centers. Floral preservative is typically a combination of sugars and antibacterial agents. The professional florist community is divided as to whether benefit is derived from preservatives. I have heard recommendations ranging from aspirin to lemon-lime soda. The commercially prepared preservatives seem to be of value but can be expensive and difficult to find. By far the best way is to start with *clean* containers and to keep that water clean and fresh by adding two to three drops of household chlorine bleach to one gallon of water. This very dilute bleach solution keeps the bacterial population in check—simply and affordably. Use it for conditioning, arranging in vases and other containers and filling the containers after the bouquet is arranged to keep it fresh.

For Sparkling Vases

Clean vases are the key to long-lasting cut-flower arrangements. The best way to keep vases clean is to change the water in the vase frequently to avoid bacteria buildup. Too often we allow the water in a vase of fresh flowers to die along with the flowers. In discarding a vase of dead flowers, you will frequently see murky green, malodorous liquid. The liquid was water but is now a bacterial slurry that has coated the interior of the vase. Simple glass bowls and wide-neck containers are relatively easy to access with sponge and scrubby. Over time, though, the more intricately molded pieces will develop a buildup of bacterial and hard-water deposits. In glass containers this makes for ugly stains that not only taint water and shorten vase life of flowers but ruin the aesthetic effectiveness of the vase. Simple cleaning may start with a bottle brush and elbow grease, but be prepared to add strong chlorine bleach solutions as found in liquid automatic dishwasher products. To reach all the nooks and crannies, try adding a small amount of coarse sand, fish gravel or fired clay kitty litter. Agitating a mixture of cleaning solution and gritty particles will clean dirt from all the crevices. Rinsed well, the container will be ready to use.

COLLECTING FLOWERS AND GREENS

Cutting from the garden offers some logistical problems. It can be difficult to bring containers of water right into the garden. In fact, doing so may slow you down, leaving the cut flowers sitting in strong sunlight. Even though they are in water, strong sunlight does more harm than the water good. I recommend bringing a small, nonbreakable container to the garden when collecting only a few flowers or greens and make a number of quick trips. Several sources offer easily transportable containers with convenient handles. For years, the basket has been used to collect flowers and greens. Though it doesn't hold water, it's light and easy to carry. If using a basket or trug, be sure to work quickly and avoid cutting during the hottest part of the day. As you pick, strip off unnecessary foliage right in the garden. Keeping a bucket or basket for compostables handy will keep the garden looking tidy. Stripping

Forsythia is among the easiest of all spring-flowering branches to force into bloom indoors. A large mass of forsythia can do much to chase away winter's gloom.

Gathering from the Wild

I often stop to collect a few blossoms from the highways and byways for inclusion in arrangements. There is something very special about some of nature's offerings to the cut flower marketplace. Queen Anne's lace, naturalized throughout the Northeast, goldenrod, the native asters and that horrible weed of wet places, purple loosestrife, all make welcome additions to the flower arranger's palette. Did I mention goldenrod? Poor goldenrod has been much maligned and is frequently confused with ragweed. Let's set the record straight: Goldenrod is not now nor has it ever been ragweed! Rag-

weed is an insignificant plant of roadsides and waste places where its green flowers produce abundant, wind-carried pollen. Goldenrod grows in the same locations, yet its pollen is heavy and not carried by the wind; rather, it requires bees to carry the pollen from blossom to blossom in order to become pollinated.

When cutting from the wild there are a few factors to take into consideration. Safety is of paramount importance, specifically when driving and parking your car. Be sure to get completely off the roadway, and as you look for a suitable place to stop and pick, don't create dangerous

situations for other drivers. Waste places that support abundant wildflowers may support other forms of wildlife, so be on the look-out for snakes, wasps, poison ivy and poison sumac, which may lead you to regret your picking expedition.

Never pick from someone's property without his or her permission. That goldenrod may be part of a planting! State laws vary, and it's best to contact the Department of Environmental Conservation or its equivalent in your state to find out which plants are protected. Don't pick protected plants unless from your own property or with permission from the

property owner. A good wildflower book is an important companion when you are collecting. Admire roadside "plantings" of wildflower mixes, but leave them for the enjoyment of others.

Harvest with moderation and consideration. Roadside flowers may be found in small pockets or colonies. When cutting from a stand of flowers it is always a good idea to leave a little behind to reseed that colony. If you remove every flower from a stand you will reduce that stand or possibly eradicate it. Good manners still dictate that we don't take the last cookie from the cookie plate.

excess foliage in the garden will lighten the load and reduce the amount of moisture loss through the foliage.

Always pick the most reliably sturdy flowers first. Don't begin with lilies and start stacking zinnias on top in your collecting basket. Flat foliage such as ferns will lie nicely in the bottom of the basket and be shaded by additions set on top. When gathering assorted treasures from the garden, such cuttings as faded blooms for potpourri and herbs for drying will be quite content if crushed under other flowers and foliage. Items such as statices and strawflowers can stand sun exposure longer if you are planning to dry them anyway. Always save the last few minutes of picking for those fragile flowers that will be ruined if crushed (lilies), or are difficult to revive if wilted (*Gaillardia* and roses).

Whenever cutting flowers, bring at least a basket, trug or container of water to carry your pickings. Even a few flowers will suffer if grasped firmly in the hand. It is amazing to me how quickly hand-held bouquets wilt, due in part to the heat emanating from the hand.

Have your conditioning containers ready for action as soon as you come in from cutting. Work quickly with the most fragile of your flowers, then with those that show signs of distress. Even if you have to get them into water before they are completely prepared, it is better to do so and go back later to finish preparing them.

Some plants produce sticky white sap, among them *Euphor-* *bia* of all types and willow *Amsonia.* Caution must be exercised when harvesting from plants with milky sap. For some people the sap can produce a mild, itchy rash. The inside of the wrist and forearm seem to be especially sensitive areas. When cutting from a plant such as *Euphorbia,* be careful with the cut ends of the stem so that both you and the other cut flowers stay clean of the sap. In arrangements, the sap will foul the water and block uptake. When you are ready to place the *Euphorbia* in the conditioning water, take a moment to sear the cut end of the stems. This can be accomplished in one of two ways. The easiest and most sensible way is to place them in a shallow container of very hot (almost boiling) water for a few moments until the sap ceases to flow. Another method involves using the open flame of a match or candle to sear the stem ends. The flame is held to the cut stem until the sap congeals. I can't help feeling that this system is not as beneficial to the bloom, though I have used it successfully in the past. Once the flow of sap has been stopped, condition the stems in warm water as you do other flower and foliage stems.

Sometimes we simply can't get everything in water quickly enough. (That is not to say we didn't try.) When greens seem lackluster or wilted, try immersing them briefly in water completely, cut stems, leaves and all. This will immediately halt any further loss of moisture and often will be enough to revive them totally. After a

Though improved varieties of goldenrod are lovely additions to the garden, this plant is abundant in many areas of the country and can be cut from roadsides and abandoned areas.

few minutes, take them out of the water, gently shake off the excess moisture, recut the stems and place the ends in a very small amount of very hot (almost boiling) water. When the water has cooled, give them a very long, deep drink of warm water overnight. Not only will the foliage perk up nicely but it will last. For delicate greens such as ivy or ferns, seal them loosely in a plastic bag after soaking and store in the refrigerator overnight. Stacking the

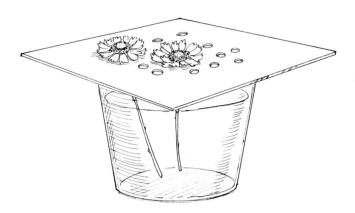

This simple device for conditioning difficult large-petaled flowers, such as daisies can be used to encourage strong, straight stems capable of supporting large flower heads.

over a deep, clean container of warm water. Prepare the flower stems and feed each stem through a hole in the cardboard. Be sure each stem extends into the water. The cardboard supports the flower, actually letting the stem hang down into the water; the flower petals are supported by the cardboard. When conditioned, the stems will be perfectly straight and the petals will be smooth and flat.

Professional florists use refrigeration to help preserve flowers in pristine condition. Most refrigerators in the home have two major problems, space and dehydration. Shorter flowers may be successfully stored in a refrigerator, yet unless carefully wrapped they will be dehydrated by the frost-free refrigerator standard on most refrigerators. Within a few hours, flowers left unwrapped in the fridge start to look like a slice of cheese left on the shelf without protection—definitely not suitable for use. As mentioned on page 31, however, make use of the refrigerator to condition greens such as ivy or fern fronds. Other flowers that can be treated the same way are flower heads harvested for garnishing or as food, among them nasturtium, *Calendula*, *Agastache* and violets. Place them on damp paper toweling in a shallow pan and cover tightly with plastic wrap. The individual blossoms will hold nicely for a day or two until you are ready to use them.

fern flat between layers of damp paper toweling will keep them perfectly shaped. Those ferns or ivy will respond nicely.

Flowers frequently come into the workroom from the garden in less than satisfactory condition. For years I had trouble saving the larger perennial daisies. Shasta daisies, *Gaillardia* and *Rudbeckia* would wilt slightly, and the flower heads would never straighten up again. We learned a trick used by commercial florists to keep *Gerbera* daisy stems strong and straight. Take a sturdy piece of cardboard and punch out numerous holes about ½ inch in diameter, in rows about 3 inches apart. Set the cardboard

FORCING

Forcing branches of spring-flowering trees and shrubs into early bloom indoors is by far one of the easiest and most rewarding things you can do. I feel guilty accepting the accolades heaped on me at Mohonk for a few simple forsythia branches gracing a hall table in February. The forcing process is quite simple. Harvest the budding branches of spring-flowering trees and shrubs. Among the easiest to force are forsythia, flowering cherry, apple, peach, pear, quince and lilac. Winter forcing doesn't work with late-spring- and summer-blooming trees and shrubs such as mock orange and hydrangea.

Prepare the harvested branches for conditioning as you would any other woody branch. Place them in a deep, clean bucket or other container and keep that container filled with plenty of clean water. To hasten the forcing process, cover the branches with a clear plastic bag and place in a well-lit area away from direct sun. In a week or two you will see flower buds begin to emerge and blossoms will start to open. The amount of time it takes blossoms to form will depend on the species harvested, the time of year (the closer it gets to their natural bloom time, the quicker it is to force), and temperature of the room where the branches are stored while being forced. If you are forcing branches for a specific occasion or holiday, start two to three weeks ahead of time and cut branches for forcing at two- to three-day intervals. If the branches are proceeding at too slow a pace, you may be able to speed up the process by soaking the entire branch in warm water in a basin or bathtub for an hour or two before replacing in the bucket of warm water. Periodically adding warm water to the forcing bucket or misting with warm water will also speed things up, as will keeping the branches in a warm environment. Beware of too much heat, which may cause buds to blast, ruining any hopes of floral display.

If you want to slow things down and hold the flowers until the day of that special dinner party, employ just the opposite techniques. Move the forced branches to a cooler location. Temperatures just above freezing (34 to 40 degrees Fahrenheit) will hold blooms for quite some time. Adding ice to the water if a cool location is not available will also slow things down considerably.

A bright wreath of summer flowers welcomes special guests to your garden. These flowers were carefully conditioned and then arranged in a wreath form made of floral foam.

DESIGNING WITH CUT FLOWERS

Good floral design is in the eye of the beholder. It has been my experience that flowers can do no wrong. That's not to say that you can't look at your work with a critical eye and improve your skills. However, it seems that no matter how dissatisfied I might be with a bouquet (even masters pull arrangements apart and start all over again), someone will come along and drool over what I felt to be absolutely horrendous.

Good flower arranging is influenced by occasion, season, function, decor, container and, most important, the arranger's likes and dislikes. As we sometimes see in the fashion magazines, haute couture and high style may not be for everyone. Some basic design rules are good to fall back on, however, when you feel something is wrong but can't put your finger on it. I avoid step-by-step how-tos because I feel they stifle imagination when you're developing a design for your home, for your color scheme and to your taste!

The basic tools of design can be easy to assemble and need not be expensive or elaborate. Let's discuss containers first. With floral foam (Oasis), containers for arrangements may be anything that will support the floral foam, whether the container holds water or not. I prefer to work without foam, as flowers last longer in lots of plain, fresh water. Therefore, I prefer containers that will hold a generous supply of water. Bowls, tall cylindrical vases, cups, mugs,

mason jars and crocks all are excellent for arrangements.

A handy type of container is actually an assortment of related vases or containers. They may be identical or merely similar in theme, shape or color. Three, five or seven small containers can be grouped together in the center of a table to make a centerpiece or set at individual dinner places as individual decorations. They may be antique medicine bottles, miniature pottery crocks, assorted small glass vases or a set of identical crystal vases. The advantage for the home-grown-flower designer is that these flower containers can be used in multiples or alone and will frequently be appropriate for small numbers of shorter flowers typically found in the garden at some times of the year.

Containers that don't hold water themselves but house water-holding vessels may be baskets, fruits and vegetables, even baked goods. If you can find a place to nestle a small container of water in an apple, you can use the apple to hold flowers. Houseplants such as philodendron and dracaena can provide a few blooms for special occasions. Such blossoms, if well conditioned, will last for a day or two when placed in well-watered potting soil. The soil will supply enough water to keep the flowers fresh; this is an old trick of commercial florists.

Remember that containers that are intricately molded are harder to clean. Some metal containers are made of materials that interact with

A dramatic mantle arrangement. Dark green candles and antique wooden fruit are an important part of this mantle arrangement which includes branches of Cornus kousa *(Japanese dogwood), green hydrangea blossoms and* Polygonum *foliage. A single brick of floral foam wrapped in plastic holds all the stems and is the "invisible" container.*

A favorite container such as this crock is equally at home with daffodils in spring and chrysanthemums in autumn. The nest of wooden robin's eggs completes the spring ensemble.

A container for an arrangement need not be a single vase. Here, six clear glass vials hold June flowers in an arrangement that can easily be re-arranged at a whim.

water, perhaps ruining the container or resulting in a chemical reaction that may shorten flower life. Brass and stainless steel are stable, but many other metals react with water or water preservatives. If in doubt, protect your container; a liner will protect the metal as well as the quality of the water. A plastic insert, old drinking glass or recycled container that holds water will work well if hidden inside the decorative container.

The shape, size and style of the container will affect the shape, size and style of the finished arrangement. Open bowls make for open, spreading arrangements. It can be difficult to arrange in open bowls without some form of mechanical device to hold stems in place. Arrangements in bowls make wonderful centerpieces, and a bowl looks quite natural on the dining table. Tall, cylindrical vases are somewhat easier to arrange in than bowls. The form an arrangement in such a vase will take is usually more upright. Vertical arrangements can be very dramatic on tall accent tables and when placed where space is at a premium, such as the lavatory cabinet. Many vases are created with a narrow base and flaring top. These V-shaped vases are easy to design in; they hold many stems, but the water reservoir is deceptively small, and this can limit flower life and encourage rapid fouling of the water. Perhaps the most versatile of all vases are the classic rose bowl and urn styles. These containers have relatively narrow necks, which

Late summer bounty is rich with the fragrance of herbs and the texture of fruits, gourds and strawberry corn. Dill and oregano flowers from the herb garden blend with other edibles.

makes for easy placement of flowers and a generous reservoir to hold plenty of fresh, clean water.

Most people find certain containers that work well for them, and that container will show up again and again over the seasons and with different displays of flowers from tulips to goldenrod. No matter what your taste, develop a collection of vases and containers, and keep them handy and clean.

Many tools will help make your job easier when the time comes to put flowers in water. A variety of devices will help hold the stems of flowers and greens in place. The most commonly used devise today is floral foam. This product has become the mainstay of the commercial florist industry. Floral foam is designed to hold many times its own weight in water and will securely hold stems of flowers and greens in place in an arrangement.

Additional devices have been designed to work with the floral foam and hold accessories such as candles or hold flowers on cake tops; they may even attach to surfaces such as mirrors. There is no doubt that it is much easier to design with floral foam, as flowers are held exactly where you place them. Foam is great to use when creating an arrangement where flowers are placed on the horizontal or even angled downward. For maximum benefit when using foam, cut it while dry so it is tall enough to extend about ½ inch above the rim of the container, and leave plenty of space in the container around the foam to add water.

Foam should be soaked thoroughly and held in place with florist's adhesive tape, sold in flower shops, craft stores and garden centers. There are a couple of drawbacks to using foam. The simple truth is that flowers last longer in lots of clean water. Floral foam is best used only once; with each additional use, the bacteria level in the foam increases and will hinder water uptake in flowers. When placing flowers in foam, be decisive; many changes in stem placement will cause the foam to break apart. When changing the angle or direction of a stem in foam, always take the stem completely out of the foam and reinsert it. Lifting a stem part way out of the foam will leave an air space at the bottom of the stem, and the flower will wilt and die.

If the floral foam that holds an arrangement is allowed to dry slightly, the flowers will suffer. Because floral foam is so adept at holding water, it will actually draw water away from the flowers and greens in an arrangement when it starts to dry out. Be sure to add plenty of good, clean water to your arrangement daily when using floral foam.

Pin holders are round or oval weighted bases that support vertical pins. The pins impale the stems of flowers and greens to hold them in place. This works extremely well with medium-size, soft stems, but pin holders are more difficult to use with woody stems or very fine, thin stems. Perhaps the most frustrating limitation when using pin holders is that it is very difficult to place stems in a ho-

A delicate crystal bowl inspires a mass arrangement of tulips and Amalanchier, *perfect on a lace cloth. The open bowl helps provide the "line" for the composition.*

The classic urn in miniature. The little glass vase is a perfect size for the average garden flower and can be used at any time of year.

rizontal plane. Although some recommend pin holders be held in place in the container using florist's clay, I find this isn't necessary as the weight of the holder is enough to secure most arrangements quite nicely. In general, I try to use a minimum of mechanics. It makes cleanup easier. Adhesive tape, florist's clay and other sticky devices can be difficult to clean off containers. A well-balanced arrangement won't need a lot of extra support. If an arrange-

Tulips combined in a free-flowing line. Lighter buds high in the arrangement add height without making the composition top-heavy. Foliage and flowers spilling over the edge of the container help to maintain a cohesive look.

This nosegay of tulips with the tiny flowers of Amalanchier *and cherry combine to create the feel of a gentler time.*

ment will be exposed to a breeze, is to be transported or moved frequently, it may then be desirable to use adhesive or clay.

Other devices have been developed to aid the flower arranger in holding flowers in a vase. There is a whole family of gadgets called "frogs," which may be wire cages, lead weights with holes in them and glass molded with holes to accept stems. All of these devices are helpful to some degree. (The holes of glass or metal frogs may be too large or small for some stems.) Their value depends on the effect you are trying to achieve. Additional materials that work well as design aids are balled-up chicken wire fencing, loosely crumpled aluminum foil, marbles or stones and twigs. Chicken wire is useful to keep on hand. You can wrap a block of floral foam with chicken wire for added support, or tape it flat over the top of a vase. Twigs cut in short lengths can be used to fill the vase somewhat and support the stems of flowers or foliage as you design. Using twigs in arrangements adds to the bulk of plant material and increases the risk of introducing bacteria and fouling the water, thereby reducing the vase life of your flowers.

The best approach with frogs and other holding devices is to use them just to get started. The first few stems of any arrangement are the most difficult to place and hold in position. Eventually, the stems will support each other and behave as you want them to. You can be successful with pinhold-

ers and frogs even in bowls, if you allow other stems in the arrangement to become part of the support mechanism of the arrangement. Even the lip of the container can support flowers and greens. The cardinal rule in flower arranging is that the cut end of the stem must be in water, the more water the better!

Let's look at some of the principles of design as they relate to flower arranging. As I've said, I don't follow them slavishly, but I refer to them when "troubleshooting" for an arrangement. When designing, I start with a container that pleases me and choose from the flowers at hand. Occasionally, I'm inspired as I pick and work an arrangement around a particular piece of vine, twig or special blossoms from a favorite plant. In the process of arranging, I simply start combining collected elements. As I approach completion, I may feel uncomfortable with the composition, and that is when I consider the elements of good design.

Proportion (scale) in flower arranging is important. The flowers and leaves should interact in a pleasing way not only together but with the container and their surroundings too. A bouquet of peonies might be a lovely composition but completely out of place when used in a small sitting area. A small demitasse cup of violets would be ridiculous as the centerpiece at a table for eight. Proportion can go awry when the flowers or foliage are out of synch with the container. A small crystal vase filled with

Visual weight is an important part of design. Dark colors carry more "weight" than their lighter-colored counterparts. The deep orange/red of the zinnia and gaillardia are placed low, while the bright yellow coreopsis is placed higher in the grouping.

delicate subjects is delightful, but the addition of a large, overbearing hosta leaf disturbs the scale. The rule of thumb is that the largest dimension of an arrangement should be about 1½ to 2 times the largest dimension of the container or vase that holds it. If this proportion is greatly exceeded or grossly underachieved, the container and arrangement will not look as though they belonged together.

To maintain proportion, the visual weight of the individual elements is important. Dark-colored elements appear heavier than light-colored elements of the same size. Light-colored flowers may appear slightly larger than dark blossoms of the same size. Place smaller, lighter flowers higher up in an arrangement and concentrate darker, larger blossoms closer to the base of the arrangement. This helps define the focal point, or visual center, of an arrangement. It appeals to our natural sense of proportion and helps develop a comfortable effect of balance, line and rhythm.

Balance is another easily understood, important element of design. I frequently use actual physical weight and balance as a guide to design. This works especially well when I use small mechanical devices to anchor my stems as the devices become the fulcrum of my balance. The tallest elements of the arrangement should counterbalance each other to keep the composition from toppling. Use visually—and physically—lighter elements such as buds and tiny flowers in the extremities of an arrangement. By concentrating the heavier flowers close to the base of an arrangement you create the impression of stability. This improves the overall composition and balance.

Line is a scary concept to some, yet it is an easy design principle to master. Line is simply the spatial relationship of individual elements to each other. The archenemy of line in design is even numbers. This is not to say that I haven't created many successful arrangements using four tulips. But, even numbers of like items in an arrangement will draw the eye toward them, and our carefully trained eyes will start to identify geometric shapes. Two red roses seem to have an imaginary line drawn between them, four will create a very nice box. In flower arrangements, these

geometric shapes are overpowering and take away from the composition. Odd numbers of flowers, arranged in threes, fives, sevens and so on, usually behave nicely and create a natural, comfortable line.

Avoid placing any two identical elements in line in either a perfectly horizontal or vertical plane. Despite the use of odd numbers in total, the eye seeks out the horizontal or vertical line and focuses on it. Instead, place one bloom slightly lower and to the left or right to break up the lines. Avoiding an overpowering line is easy.

Rhythm is related to line and is most important in arrangements that rely on the placement of few blossoms for effect. In a line arrangement, a limited number of flowers are used to create a balanced design, so the flowers must be selected carefully. Flowers lead the eye from blossom to blossom toward the focal point. The simple effect of a good design is deceptive, because success with the line arrangement requires careful positioning of individual blossoms. Using the principles of proportion, balance and line help achieve the rhythm necessary for success in a line arrangement.

Color is fun, and we shouldn't have to worry about suitable color combinations in flower arranging. It is in regard to color that I too often hear the *can't* word. Some people feel that no one should use blue vases (why do they make blue vases then?). Others insist you can't combine pink with orange or red with purple. Let me take this opportunity to set

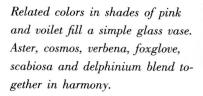

The placement of garden flowers in this monochromatic composition makes for a naturalistic grouping. Using flowers of different sizes and increasing the density of color at the base of the arrangement create balance and a focal point.

Related colors in shades of pink and voilet fill a simple glass vase. Aster, cosmos, verbena, foxglove, scabiosa and delphinium blend together in harmony.

the record straight. You can combine any colors successfully in floral design and can use any vase or container without disastrous results.

Horticulturally, there is no pure color. Crayon hues of pure orange, red, yellow and blue don't exist. Close examination of white flowers will show highlights of green, yellow, white or pink. Pinks are frequently blushed with coral or violet, even green. Yellows may have undertones of green or orange. And blue, well, blue is a very difficult color to find without some hint of violet. All this is a blessing in disguise. Color combinations are suggested within each blossom. Look toward the center, the base of the petals, the exterior of the petals or at the stamens and pistils, and you will see colors to which the flower is related. Introducing those colors to the arrangement will create wonderful harmony.

Green is the one constant in floral design. Even without adding the foliage of ferns or shrubbery, the various greens of stems and the natural leaves of each blossom introduce green to an arrangement. Green in the landscape or in the vase is an effective unifying element. The foliage of plants comes in an amazing assortment of colors, and greens can vary greatly. Green can be dark or light and have blue, yellow or red overtones. Foliage may be green, gray or variegated in any number of combinations from the vertical striping of ribbon grass to the almost-perfect golden edging of some hosta. The color of the variegation varies, too, yellow and green being the most common; green and white, green and silver, and tricolor variegations as in the tricolor sage are all suitable for inclusion in arrangements.

Color is a matter of personal taste and should be influenced by decor, vase and table linens (if any). Sometimes people feel the season or occasion dictates the colors used: white for weddings; pastels for Easter and baby showers; red and green for Christmas holiday festivities; and yellow, golds and russets in the autumn. Colors may be arranged together with like colors to create a monochromatic scheme, or with color opposites to develop a complementary color scheme. Blue and orange are complements, as are yellow and lavender, and red and green. Color "neighbors" work well together: russet with orange and yellow, blue with lavender and pink. Polychromatic color combinations are vivid blendings of a range of colors, bringing together the primary hues of red, yellow and blue with oranges, pinks, whites and violets for a riot of color. For pleasing color combinations, you should do as you like, not as some "expert" advises.

Try not to think of arranging as the art of vase decoration. I am very fond of and often choose to use a softly hued, medium green bowl. Glass containers are, of course, a noncolor choice. White and black containers too frequently can become integral parts of the designs. Black can be very elegant and commanding of attention and calls for a dramatic sense of color in the arrangement. Colored vases by their very nature should become an

A small sampling of foliage from the garden. From top center, clockwise: Mountain laurel, viburnum, dusty miller, hay-scented fern, variegated weigelia, 'Purple Ruffles' basil, gardener's ribbon grass and Canadian hemlock.

A sampling of color in arrangements, from left to right: analogous shades of pink asters, carmine cosmos, and violet verbena and delphinium; complementary orange tithonia and blue salvia; complementary red Cardinal flower and red crab apples with assorted foliages; complementary yellow goldenrod and zinnia with lavender asters; anagolous yellow coreopsis with orange zinnias and gaillardia; and monochromatic white on white balloon flowers, snapdragons, asters, Queen Anne's lace and scabiosa.

Beauty and fragrance in the bedroom. Roses and lavender provide scent in the bouquet of mixed flowers of early summer. Lupine, columbine, mullein pink, allium and slender deutzia complete the arrangement.

A play for texture. Soft, feathery blooms combine with the rich texture of velvety rose petals in an old basket. The gardener's ribbon grass provides line and textural interest as well.

Scent in Bouquets

I have frequently said that I garden as much with my nose as my hands. Gardening and flower arranging are joys to all the senses. The nose shouldn't be ignored. Incorporating scent in an arrangement is not a prerequisite of good design, but it should often be a consideration. Many flowers and foliages provide scent for bouquets. Here are a few of my favorites: Lilies of the valley, mignonettes, scented geraniums, basils and other herbs, garden pinks and carnations, lilacs, roses, sweet peas, lavenders (foliage and flowers), lilies, nicotianas, peonies, phloxes and sweet bay magnolias. Not all scents are for everyone. Boxwood foliage and marigolds offend some people, and strongly scented flowers may become overpowering in small, enclosed spaces.

integral part of the color scheme of the design and demand the designer tie it together in some way.

Texture is the "color" of feel. In arrangements we experience texture visually and relate it to a tactile experience we recognize. We can visualize rough, smooth, velvety, glossy and spiny. Variation of texture enhances arrangements. By combining rough with smooth or velvety with glossy, another dimension comes into play. The use of texture is critical in a monochromatic scheme in which slight variations in color can be emphasized by contrasting textures.

Depth is a consideration in flower arranging as we are working with three-dimensional objects. Unfortunately, all too often we find that all the elements of an composition have been placed in one plane. This sort of design might have everything else going for it, but it misses depth. By layering flowers and foliage in the design, you can increase the interest level of the arrangement. Look at a garden. Are all of the flowers planted in a single row? Do all of the flowers face the same way? Of course not. A garden is three dimensional. The flowers are layered, and as you walk past, you see a slightly different composition from your changing perspective. The changing combinations of colors, textures and

Muted tones of cream, blue and yellow-green with the rich accents of foliage provide a delightful combination. The depth of flower placement helps to maintain the three-dimensional appearance even in a photograph.

Lilies should be a part of every cutting garden. The velvety colors are combined with dill, tansy and Klondike cosmos. When designing with lilies it is wise to remove the pollen-bearing anthers, as the pollen can stain.

lines are exciting. For an arrangement with depth, flowers are placed in the design at different levels, yet each is shown off to good advantage at different angles and when seen from various heights.

Mechanics is the term used by flower arrangers for the devices to secure the flowers. I don't often use them, though I sometimes use a frog or pin holder to anchor the first few stems to give me a head start with a design. The nasty thing about mechanics is that they must be camouflaged so they do not disrupt the beauty of the design. The most common means of hiding mechanics is to cover them with adequate foliage. In some instances, however, greens are not the answer. Other means of covering floral foam, pin holders or frogs is with Spanish or sphagnum moss (available at garden centers and craft shops), stones or marbles, shells, and even blossoms themselves. Whatever material is used should be clean so as not to foul the water (critical in the case of clear glass containers, where dirty water is immediately evident). Be leery of substances that become malodorous when in contact with water or produce a substance toxic to flowers and greens.

Our friends the flowers can be idiosyncratic. Not all behave as they should. Tulips, those delights of the spring garden and vase, are wonderful subjects when cut except for one minor problem, the tendency to grow. Tulips continue to grow in the vase and will, if allowed to do so, extend beyond the other flowers they were arranged with. There is no helping this phenomenon except to lift them out and cut back the ends of the stems. The flower petals will also open and close with the coming and going of daylight. I stop this bad habit by making a small vertical cut just below the flower head about ½ inch long and deep enough to reach about halfway into the stem.

Another flower that may disrupt the orderliness of your floral design is the snapdragon. Snapdragons are one of the best cut flowers, unparalleled in color and scent, but they have wayward tips. The last two or three inches of each snapdragon will reach upward. This is not an especially bothersome habit but it can turn a lovely centerpiece into something that more closely resembles Liberace's candelabrum.

Lilies don't move, grow or change once arranged, but lily pollen does seem to have a mind of its own. Most professional florists remove the pollen. It is a shame to have to do so because the nodding, pollen-heavy anthers add a certain charm. The sad truth is that lily pollen stains, sometimes permanently. Unless you are putting an arrangement in a safe place away from brushing sleeves and curious noses, I recommend removing the anthers. Use a tissue to grasp the pollen-bearing anther and pull gently—it's rather like blowing a child's nose. If you should inadvertently get pollen on a garment or tablecloth, resist the urge to brush it away immediately. Allow the pollen to dry for an hour or more, then lightly brush it away or use the vacuum cleaner.

Maintaining the flower arrangement is an integral part of success with home-grown cut flowers. Once the flowers have been arranged to your satisfaction, keep the arrangement looking good! Some locations in the home are ideal for placing cut flowers, some less so. It is never a good idea to mix flowers in water with electrical equipment such as televisions or entertainment systems. An accidental spill could cause an expensive repair or create a dangerous electrical shock. At Mohonk we never place arrangements on pianos or other musical instruments; experience has taught us that accidental spills of water can cause expensive repairs.

Avoid heat and direct sun with flower arrangements. Locations near fireplaces, radiators and strong, hot lighting all shorten the life of and enjoyment you'll receive from flowers. Flowers will do best in a cool room with adequate ventilation, but away from strong air currents and drafts.

Most florists finish a bouquet with a thorough misting with a spray bottle. Misting an arrangement not only keeps the flowers and foliages looking fresh but will help an arrange-ment last longer. The mist reduces moisture loss through the petals and leaves. In an overly warm house or apartment, misting will cool the flowers and, as the water evaporates, increase the humidity in the room.

The most common cause of failure with flower arrangements is lack of water. Ideally, all the stems of flowers and greens are well immersed in water. This isn't always the case, though, because to achieve the proper angle or use that special but short-stemmed rose, some stems are in only one or two inches of water. Adding water daily will maintain water level and help keep the water in the vase fresh. Use warm water to refresh most arrangements. However, to add hours to the enjoyment of bowls of cut spring-flowering bulbs such as tulips and daffodils, add a handful of ice cubes to help cool the arrangement and add water as they melt.

Some flowers last longer in the vase than others. As a flower begins to fade you may be able to eliminate it or replace it and continue to enjoy the rest of the bouquet for days afterward. Rather than try to pull out the spent bloom, cut it out as close to the vase as possible. Pulling a flower stem out of an arrangement may disrupt the entire composition.

A Word About Style

Several personalities have recently become big promoters of their "style." It's a great word and a wonderful concept. I have always felt it is more important to be comfortable than stylish, and our home reflects that philosophy. Preferences in styles and trends change dramatically over time (who would have thought the miniskirt would return?). What do not change are your personality and your love of fresh flowers. When arranging flowers in your kitchen or work room, do so because you enjoy doing so. If you want to mimic the great designers of the day, do it! Copying from fashion magazines or decorating books can be great fun.

Whatever style you choose, remember to be comfortable with your designs, enjoy the combination of gardening and bringing the garden indoors and wallow in the glory of a garden well tended, a bountiful harvest and the beauty you and nature helped create.

PLANT PORTRAITS

It has been difficult to limit the number of plants discussed in these plant portraits because an unlimited number of plants lend themselves to cutting and enjoying indoors. Anyone who has grown and harvested flowers for arranging will undoubtedly be perturbed with me for eliminating some special favorite. I have chosen plants that are valued for their size, shape, texture and lasting ability as well as those that may offer a specific challenge for the gardener or designer. The Plant Portraits represent all of the major horticultural groups: trees, shrubs, ornamental and edible plants and, of course, the annuals, biennials and perennials. As you use this book, you will find I have recommended species and varieties not described in the plant portraits; for many of these, specific information on their cultural requirements and landscape use can be found in other Burpee American Gardening Series books.

My father once said that you have to learn from the mistakes of others because you don't have enough time to make them all yourself. I encourage you to learn from my experience and mistakes, and hope this broadens your horizons enough so you learn from your future experiences.

The plants that follow are listed by their botanic names and cross-referenced by their common names. Common names, though easier to pronounce and frequently endearing (who can resist love-in-a-mist?) vary from area to area, but botanic names are understood from Boston to Bangkok. Botanic names are listed by the genus and include species and sometimes subspecies or cultivar names. Cultivar—cultivated variety—names usually appear in single quotation marks.

PLANT PORTRAIT KEY

Here is a guide to the symbols and terms used throughout this section.

Latin name of the plant is in boldface italic.

Phonetic pronunciation of the Latin name is in parentheses.

Common name of the plant is in boldface type.

The average hours of sun needed per day is indicated by symbols. The first symbol is what the plant prefers, but the plant is adaptable to all conditions listed.

○ *Sun*—Six hours or more of strong, direct sunlight per day.

◐ *Part shade*—Three to six hours of direct sunlight per day.

● *Shade*—Two hours or less of direct sunlight per day.

◗ *Drought resistant*

✳ *Heat lover*

✳ *Cool weather preference*

H *Condition in hot water (150 degrees Fahrenheit).*

W *Condition in warm water (100 to 120 degrees Fahrenheit).*

C *Condition in cool water (room temperature).*

S *Special conditioning requirements.*

Zones: Check the Plant Hardiness Map (pages 92-93), based on average annual temperature for each area—or zone—of the United States to see what zone you live in. Every plant portrait lists the zones best for that plant.

Whether it's exquisite foliage, charming buds or beautiful blossoms, every flower has something to offer the flower arranger. Penstemon has a delightful presence in the garden and makes a wonderful addition to any arrangement.

ANNUALS

Antirrhinum majus *are among the best cutting flowers, easy to grow and easy to harvest successfully. Pinch young plants to encourage basal branching.*

Amaranthus caudatus, *the quintessential romantic flower for bouquets.*

Ageratum houstonianum (aj-er-AY-tum hew-stōn-ee-AH-num) **blue flossflower,** ○ ◐ ✳ **W**

Characteristics: Ageratum is an old-fashioned, annual favorite known mostly for its value as a bedding plant. Fuzzy lavender-blue flowers are borne in clusters on top of medium-length stems. The typically compact, 8- to 10-inch plants are the result of much breeding, and today's *Ageratum* is not the *Ageratum* of our grandmothers. Avoid bedding varieties for cutting, and look for the *Ageratum* still available in heights of 20 to 30 inches.

Cultural Information: Ageratum does best in full sun in rich, well-drained garden soils, but it will produce good-quality cutting stems in light shade. *Ageratum* has few insect or disease problems. Seed in place after last frost or start indoors on a sunny windowsill about six weeks before last frost. The best *Ageratum* varieties for cutting are 'Bavaria' and 'Blue Horizon'.

Harvest and Use: In bouquets, *Ageratum* does very well with yellow roses (try 'Sunbright'), zinnias and snapdragons. It

Ageratum, *with its delightful, lavender-blue flowers, is available in heights of 24 to 30 inches, excellent for cutting. Try the variety 'Blue Horizon'.*

may be difficult to blend successfully with oranges and golden yellows.

Amaranthus (am-a-RAN-thus) **amaranth,** ○ ✳ ◆ **H**

Characteristics: The amaranths comprise a group of frequently overlooked annuals that are wonderful additions to the annual border and the cutting garden. Several varieties available from seed are delightful garden performers, producing excellent cutting flowers and foliage. *A. caudatus,* also known as love-lies-bleeding and kiss-me-over-the-garden-gate, is characterized by long, weeping panicles of fuzzy burgundy flowers. The effect of these flowers is quite dramatic whether used fresh or dried. *A. caudatus* 'Scarlet Torch', producing shorter, upright spikes to 12 inches, is another heat- and sun-loving annual. It is effective used either fresh or dried.

Cultural Information: Amaranths are grown easily from seed sown in soils in spring after the danger of frost is past, or started indoors 6 weeks before planting outdoors. They thrive in well-drained soils of average fertility. Taller varieties may need staking.

Harvest and Use: It is best to remove all foliage before conditioning. Love-lies-bleeding is handsome when arranged to weep over the edge of a pedestal vase and puddle gently on the table below. Or arrange it on a mantle, letting it hang to its full length. The muted, deep red ropes blend well with many

different colors and textures. Try it with orange lilies and deep green hosta foliage. The shorter, rust-colored spires of *A. c.* 'Scarlet Torch' combine well with the bright oranges of marigolds and cosmos, providing lovely textural and color counterpoint.

Annual aster; see *Callistephus*

Annual baby's breath; see *Gypsophila elegans*

Annual larkspur; see *Consolida*

Antirrhinum majus (anti-RY-num MAH-yus) **snapdragon,** ○ ◐ ✳ **W**

Characteristics: The snapdragon is essential to the cutting garden. The offering of colors from pure white to deep burgundy and pale yellow to bronze and orange give the gardener a wonderful color range. The full-bodied spikes of delicate florets can be grown in two forms: the closed-mouth "dragon style" and the bright, open-faced type such as 'Madame Butterfly'. For maximum height and color selection of the standard snapdragon form, the best choices are from the 'Rocket Series'.

Cultural Information: The seeds are easy to germinate in cool temperatures. Seedlings of Rocket "snaps" are available at many garden centers and nurseries in spring. When seedlings are about 4 inches tall and have several sets of leaves, pinch out the uppermost set of leaves and terminal bud to produce stockier, well-branched plants; they will perform better in the garden.

Harvest and Use: Harvesting spikes of snapdragons will encourage basal branching and more flower stems will be produced. Cut stems should be stripped of foliage before conditioning in warm water. An upright placement in an arrangement is more pleasing than a horizontal placement, as the tips of snaps continue to grow toward the light. All snapdragon colors are valuable, but one of my favorites is 'Rocket Series' bronze. Close inspection of this bronze flower reveals pink, yellow and orange overtones, making it ideal for blending with a wide range of flowers including blue *Salvia*, cosmos and lisianthus.

Aster, China; see **_Callistephus_**

Baby's breath, annual; see **_Gypsophila elegans_**

Bachelor's button; see **_Centaurea_**

Bells of Ireland; see **_Moluccella_**

Blue flossflower; see **_Ageratum_**

Blue lace flower; see **_Trachymene_**

Blue throatwort; see **_Trachelium_**

Calendula officinalis

(ka-LEN-dew-la ŏf-fish-in-AL-is) **pot marigold,** ○ ◑ ✳ **C**

Characteristics: Pot marigold is a wonderful, long-lasting cutting flower that is also one of the best of the edible flowers. This easy-to-grow annual blooms well throughout the season and produces numerous flowers for harvesting. Several improved varieties are available with colors ranging from cream to apricot. 'Pacific' at 24 inches provides stems suitable for cutting. As with other annuals, calendula responds well to cutting by producing more flowers.

Cultural Information: Calendula is extremely easy to grow and will thrive in almost any soil. Sow seed in early spring as soon as soil can be worked. Thin seedlings to six to eight inches apart to provide adequate room for proper development. Pot marigolds like plenty of moisture and benefit from a midseason fertilizer application.

Harvest and Use: Cut stems of *Calendula* should be placed in cool water until you are ready to design; they are easy to condition. The yellows of pot marigolds are among the purest of all yellow flowers, and combined with purple larkspur, it's dynamite.

Calendula *bright yellow or golden orange flowers are at home in fresh flower arrangements useful in potpourri, and excellent when tossed in a green salad.*

Callistephus chinensis *will fill late-summer and early-autumn bouquets with strong shades of blue, violet, red, rose, pink and white in single and double flowering forms.*

Callistephus chinensis

(ka-LEE-ste-fus chy-NEN-sis) **China (annual) aster,** ○ **W**

Characteristics: The China or annual aster is one of the most prized annual flowers for bouquets and arranging. Asters come in a range of lovely colors from crystal white to deep, pure blue; shades of palest pink to deep burgundy fill out the spectrum. Asters are available in single, daisylike and fully double forms. 'Totem Pole', 'Powder Puff Bouquet' and 'Single Rainbow' demonstrate the full range of colors and a diversity of bloom sizes from the two-inch 'Powder Puff' to the four-inch 'Totem Pole'. When choosing varieties, look for a statement of wilt resistance, as aster wilt can devastate your crop. Asters bloom in late summer and are the backbone of the August and September cutting garden.

Cultural Information: Aster is easy to grow from seed and does well in most garden soils. Local greenhouses and garden centers usually offer an assortment of varieties each spring; avoid dwarf bedding asters that don't produce stems suitable for cutting. Thin asters 10 inches apart in well-prepared soil enriched with organic matter. Incorporate a balanced fertilizer into the soil before planting, and side-dress with additional fertilizer when flower buds begin to develop in July. Asters tolerate drought, but irrigation during dry periods will result in larger and superior blooms. Taller varieties should be staked in windy areas.

Harvest and Use: Asters combine well with many other cut flowers, and their straight, sturdy stems make them wonderfully easy for designing. Combine them with burgundy snapdragons, blue lisianthus and white phlox for a lovely late-summer bouquet.

Celosia argentea (se-LO-see-a ar-GEN-tee-a) **cockscomb,** ○ ◑ ◗ ❋ **W**

Characteristics: Cockscombs are grown in two forms, each one worthwhile in small quantities in the cutting garden. Both forms are lovely garden specimens, providing long-lasting blossoms ideal for use fresh

Celosia *are bright, reliable additions to the annual cutting garden or integrated garden. They can be used fresh or dried for everlasting bouquets.*

Centaurea cyanus *is a favorite from Victorian times. The brilliant, clear blue combines well with many other flowers, but don't neglect the other colors: white, pale pink through rose, and maroon.*

and dried. Cockscombs are available in many rich colors from red to yellow, including deep burgundy and orange. *Celosia argentea plumosa* or the plumed cockscomb has been the subject of much breeding work during the past several years, resulting in stockier, more dwarf plants. This does not always benefit the flower arranger. A highlight of the 1993 garden season is the new variety 'Flamingo Feather', growing to 24 inches and topped with a much smaller, more delicate version of the typical plumed cockscomb. 'Flamingo Feather' is a pleasant medium pink in color and an exciting textural contrast to some of its more staid garden colleagues such as lilies, roses, daisies and cosmoses. *Celosia argentea* 'New Look', 'Apricot Brandy' and 'Golden Triumph' are varieties worth including in the cutting garden. Dried blossoms will last for months and their velvety colors will enrich autumn bouquets and holiday arrangements.

Celosia argentea cristata, the crested cockscomb, is quite different from the plumed cockscomb. The crested cockscombs grow in undulating fans and form heads as they mature. Crested cockscomb is wonderful used fresh in late-summer and autumn bouquets and in dried arrangements year 'round. The texture is velvety, the colors deep and rich. The Burpee 'Floradale Series' in mixed colors is an excellent quality cockscomb.

Cultural Information: Cockscomb is an easy-to-grow annual that thrives in warm soils and full sun. A wide choice of vari-

eties is usually available from the nursery or garden center each spring. Choose seedlings—from the greenhouse or garden center, or when growing your own from seed—that are actively growing, and make sure the young growth is not checked in the seedling flat. Look for young, vigorous plants that are not yet fully blooming. Foliage will not always be a deep green; plants with paler blooms frequently have pale or chartreuse foliage. Some of the reds have lovely burgundy foliage that sets off the bright flowers nicely in both garden and vase.

Harvest and Use: Condition cockscombs in warm water after removing all but the uppermost pair of leaves. Plumed cockscomb looks lovely combined with coreopsis and the strong-colored autumn mums. Crested cockscomb adds a great wealth of color and texture to any bouquet. For a festive holiday or harvest-time arrangement, arrange cockscomb in a hollowed-out pumpkin and surround with assorted gourds and Indian corn.

Centaurea cyanus (sent-OW-ree-a see-AH-nus) **bachelor's buttons, cornflowers,** ○ ❋ ◗ **W**

Characteristics: Centaurea cyanus is a standard of the cutting garden. Although most noted for the wonderful blue (cornflower blue!), shades of white, pink, violet and burgundy complete the color range, all of them desirable in the cutting garden and vase. 'Polka Dot' offers a full range of colors and produces nice, straight stems for cutting.

Centaurea is a large genus of several annuals and perennials, many of which are suitable for cutting. *C. moschata* is known as sweet sultan. The flowers are the same size as those of bachelor's buttons but appear as softer, rounded, powder-puff blooms. The colors range from white to lavender, all soft pastel shades.

Cultural Information: Seed bachelor's buttons where they are to grow in well-prepared garden soil. A full-sun location in well-drained soils will benefit *Centaurea*, which does not require extremely rich soils. Like some of the other garden favorites, bachelor's buttons will reseed themselves, and for the lazy gardener they will reappear year after year. In the garden, beware of powdery mildew, a death knell to these flowers not fond of heat and humidity. Regular harvesting of blossoms for fresh use and drying keeps the plants producing throughout the season. Staking may be necessary if they are grown in fertile ground. Avoid shade and crowded areas in the garden, which might further predispose bachelor's buttons to mildew problems.

Harvest and Use: It may be tedious to pull the leaves off the stems of bachelor's buttons, but this will reward you by keeping the water fresh and clean. Both bachelor's buttons and sweet sultan will serve you well in the vase for two weeks or longer if the water remains clean. I like the bright, pure blue of cornflowers with the pure yellow of coreopsis and bright orange Klondyke cosmos. *Centaurea* combines well

with many spring-flowering and early-summer favorites.

China aster; see ***Callistephus***

Cockscomb; see ***Celosia***

Common garden cosmos; see ***Cosmos***

Consolida orientalis
(kon-SO-li-da o-ree-en-TAL-is) **annual larkspur,** ○ ◑ ✳ **W**

Characteristics: Larkspur provides one of the valuable blues of the cutting garden. The tall flower spikes are also available in white and pink shades and grow to four feet. 'Giant Imperial' is a mix of all the larkspur colors, and one packet of seeds will provide many cuts for fresh and dried use.

Cultural Information: Larkspur prefers cool temperatures, and by giving it a head start in spring you will have larger spikes and a longer season of bloom. To get the jump on spring, sow larkspur seed where they are to grow in the fall. Mark the location carefully so the garden spot is not tilled or inadvertently weeded out. Larkspur will need staking in exposed locations; use a medium-weight bamboo cane, and tie at about one foot and again 10 to 12 inches higher.

Harvest and Use: Larkspur dries nicely, holding its color into the winter, but it is the bright, elegant stems in fresh bouquets that makes it most valuable. 'Giant Imperial' is reliable, large and guaranteed to produce an abundance of cutting material. Be sure to re-

move all the ferny foliage when preparing for conditioning. Larkspur will last for 7 to 10 days in water. Try combining larkspur with roses for a traditional look or with masses of cosmos for a carefree arrangement. Care should be taken when handling the seeds and foliage of *Consolida* as they are poisonous.

Cornflower; see ***Centaurea***

Cosmos (KOS-mos) **common garden cosmos,** ○ ✳ ◗ **W**

Characteristics: Cosmos bipinnatus is an old-fashioned favorite that deserves space in any garden. The 'Sensation Series' is the most common form available, but 'Seashells' is an interesting variation, with its petals curved into shell or funnel shapes around the golden centers. *C. bipinnatus* comes in wonderful shades from pure white to carmine, with many gently striped and shaded forms available. Breeders are working on a pale yellow form that will be an interesting addition to our cutting garden at

Consolida orientalis *'Giant Imperial Mixed' is easily grown from seed and will provide ample cuts if seed is sown in autumn or very early spring. You'll want plenty for fresh and dry use.*

Plant Cosmos bipinnatus *in the background where they will not shade smaller plants. If allowed to reseed themselves, Cosmos will form a larger clump with additional flowers for bouquets.*

Dianthus barbatus *is noted for its sweetly fragrant flower heads. Many ruffled and bicolor forms exist. Get the taller varieties, as dwarf forms may prove difficult to cut.*

Digitalis purpurea *is a true biennial, but 'Foxy' will bloom the first year from seed if sown early. The delicate spires of flowers add elegance to any arrangement.*

Mohonk. Cosmos are large-boned members of the garden, growing to five feet, with flowers up to 3½ inches across. The foliage is a soft ferny green.

C. sulphureus, the Klondyke cosmos, is a shorter, hotter-colored relative of *C. bipinnatus*. *C. sulphureus* has stiffer, almost marigoldlike foliage and grows to 24 to 30 inches, depending on variety. It produces a large number of flowers with 8- to 10-inch stems in colors from yellow to deep red.

Cultural Information: In the garden both cosmos forms described above require full sun, well-drained soil and moderate fertility. Too much fertilizer early in the season will delay bloom. If allowed to reseed, *C. bipinnatus* will return to the garden year after year, creating an ever-changing display of pink, white, magenta and carmine hues. It is always wise to stake cosmos early in the season with a heavy-duty bamboo cane or other suitable support.

Harvest and Use: Cosmos provides good, long cutting stems if you are not afraid to sacrifice some buds—buds look great in the flower arrangement. 'Sensation Series' cosmoses will last for 1 or more weeks in the vase if conditioned in warm water. The pink, deep rose and white blooms can be used with the blue of *Trachelium* and with larkspur to great advantage. The Klondykes are reliable and will last well if cut early. They shatter (petals fall rapidly off blossom) when past their prime. The colors are clean and clear. One of my all-time favorite combinations is orange cosmos with blue *Salvia*.

Dianthus barbatus (dee-ANTH-us bar-BA-tus) **sweet William,** ○ ✳ **C**

Characteristics: The sweetly fragrant flowers of sweet Williams are borne on flattened heads. The inflorescences are like individual, single pinks (perennial *Dianthus*) in shades from white to deep pink and purple. Many of the flowers are shaded, striped, blotched or edged in contrasting colors. Avoid wet soils and crowding for the greatest success with *Dianthus*. Count on sweet William to top out at about 18 inches with stems of 12 or more inches.

Cultural Information: D. barbatus is in fact a biennial, but it can be grown as an annual if started indoors in early spring. Sweet William can be sown in late summer to early fall where they are to bloom in the spring, or indoors to be moved into the border in the spring for early summer bloom.

Harvest and Use: D. barbatus is an excellent cut flower and will hold in water for two weeks or longer if conditioned properly. Combine sweet William with blue *Salvia* and mullein pink for delightful results.

Digitalis purpurea 'Foxy' (di-ji-TAL-is pur-pew-REE-a) **foxglove,** ○ ◐ **W**

Zones: 4 to 9

Characteristics: Digitalis 'Foxy' was a breakthrough in breeding when introduced several years ago. It is the first foxglove reliable as an annual. 'Foxy' is commonly found in garden centers and greenhouses in spring. Foxgloves make excellent specimens for cutting, with graceful spikes of flowers in shades from creamy white to rosy lavender. The throats of the blooms are intricately spotted with deep purples. *D. purpurea* Excelsior hybrids have individual florets produced around the stem for a much denser spike. The species *D. × mertonensis* is a true perennial form the color of strawberry yogurt. All species of *Digitalis* are poisonous and should be handled with care.

Cultural Information: Plant in well-drained garden soil enriched with organic matter. Foxgloves do well in partial shade and produce a large number of flowers suitable for cutting. *D. purpurea* is a true biennial, requiring 2 years to complete its life cycle. Allow the best of the plants to set seed and they will self-sow; in this way they will make a lovely, self-sustaining colony.

Harvest and Use: Harvest *Digitalis* when about one-third of the blossoms are open. *Digitalis* holds nicely in water for 2 weeks or longer if conditioned in warm water overnight. Combinations with hardy lilies, roses, cosmoses, shasta daisies or other rounded forms are especially handsome. Try the more purple shades with yarrow or tansy for a pretty, complementary arrangement.

Euphorbia marginata (EW-for-bee-a mar-ji-NAH-ta) **snow-on-the-mountain,** ○ ◐ ✳ ◆ **S, H**

Characteristics: Snow-on-the-mountain is a wonderfully bright member of the poinsettia family. It is tall, bold and makes an enchanting accent in the integrated border or cutting garden. *Euphorbia* produces a sticky white sap when cut and care must be taken in handling it (see page 31). Snow-on-the-mountain produces cleanly variegated foliage of gray-green striped with purest white. The tiny white flowers add some textural interest but are insignificant.

Cultural Information: Euphorbia is a strong grower that does best in full sun and warm locations. Sow seed directly outdoors in early spring where it is to grow, as the plants don't like to be moved. Snow-on-the-mountain will grow to 3 to 4 feet, and can fill a space in the back of the mixed border. Thin young plants to about 1 foot apart to allow them adequate space to mature. Staking may be required in exposed locations.

Harvest and Use: A searing dip in water that is boiling hot or exposing the cut stems to flame will congeal the sap and keep it from fouling water in the conditioning container and vase. After searing, give them a deep drink of hot water to condition overnight. The effect when mixed with flowers of any color is outstanding. For an elegant effect, use snow-on-the-mountain in an all-white bouquet with hydrangea, white snapdragon or gladiolus and white *lisianthus*.

Eustoma grandiflorum
(yew-STO-ma gran-di-FLO-rum)
lisianthus, prairie gentian,
○ ◑ **H**

Characteristics: Eustoma grandiflorum has had a somewhat uncertain beginning. A development of plant breeders, it was first named *Lisianthus Russellianus* and may still appear under this genus. Lisianthus, a child of the prairies, has be-

come a cut flower of renown. It is available in pale shell pink, white, deep blue, rose, lilac and bicolored white with purple edges. Double varieties have been introduced in the past few years, adding to the versatility of this cut flower. The Yodel hybrid varieties have become the standards in the single types, whereas 'Lion' and 'Double Eagle' are excellent sources of the double forms of cut flowers in mixed colors. The buds are a great part of the plant's charm. Each petal swirls around the other, overlapping in a delicate pointed spiral, and the flower opens looking like a single poppy or tulip. The doubles don't have the grace of bud of the singles, nor do they possess the purity of form when open. They do provide a long-lasting, roselike flower that is very elegant in any flower arrangement.

Cultural Information: Eustoma is slow to germinate and sometimes fussy in the seed flat. Unless you have ideal growing conditions to start seedlings indoors early, you may be better off buying started seedlings from a greenhouse in spring. It takes about 140 days for flowers to be produced from seed, so direct seeding is not recommended in northern climates. Plant *Eustoma* seedlings in a full-sun location in well-drained garden soil. They will tolerate drought once established, but thrive in moist, well-drained soils. Staking is generally not necessary for these plants, which reach a maximum height of 2 feet.

Harvest and Use: The flowers are borne on sprays with sturdy, smooth stems. The

Euphorbia marginata *will thrive in hot, sunny locations. When harvesting, scald the stem ends in very hot water to arrest the flow of milky sap.*

Eustoma grandiflorum *may be difficult to grow from seed, but the end result is breathtaking. Cut and placed in water, the flowers may last for three weeks in an arrangement.*

gray-green foliage stays neat and is not demanding when cut. Lisianthus is a reliable cut flower that will last for 3 weeks in a vase of water. Harvest an entire spray to get stems that are suitably long for design work or cut just the individual blooms on 4- to 6-inch stems for smaller vases. Conditioning cut stems is easy in hot water; lisianthus is almost always successful as a cut flower. Unlike some other annuals, it is slow to produce new stems, producing only three to four sprays of flowers over the course of the growing season. The primary flower will open first and be followed by a number of secondary buds. Though the buds last well in water, smaller buds will not mature when cut. Combine lisianthus with any number of other cuts for a variety of looks. The satiny petals harmonize nicely with snapdragons, stocks, sweet peas and lilies. Or provide a contrast in texture with *Astilbe,* yarrows or gayfeathers.

Flossflower; see *Ageratum*

Flowering tobacco; see ***Nicotiana***

Foxglove; see *Digitalis*

Garden sage; see *Salvia*

The cloverlike blossoms of Gomphrena globosa *will delight the gardener and flower arranger alike. Grow plenty of these drought-tolerant flowers for fresh and dry use.*

Baby's breath is easily cultivated in well-drained soil that is slightly alkaline, hence the generic name Gypsophila. *The annual 'Covent Garden White' will provide pure white flowers on graceful stems.*

Globe amaranth; see ***Gomphrena***

Gloriosa daisy; see ***Rudbekia***

Gomphrena globosa
(gom-FREE-nah glo-BO-sa) **globe amaranth,** ○ ✳ ◐ **W**

Characteristics: Globe amaranths are easy-to-grow, sun-loving annuals that are a must for every cutting garden. The rounded, cloverlike blossoms come in shades of white, pink, lavender, magenta, orange and strawberry red. Upon close inspection, the flowers appear to have reflective, shiny surfaces, but the overall effect in the garden and bouquet is that of rather coarse, bristly flowers. *G. g.* 'Buddy' was bred as a bedding plant and grows to 8 to 10 inches. Look for tall mixed strains, 'Strawberry Fayre' (or 'Strawberry Fields'), 'Lavender Queen' and *G. haageana,* which is a bright orange.

Cultural Information: There are several varieties available for growing from seed. Seedlings are purchased at the garden center or greenhouse in spring. Plant them out after danger of frost in full sun. *Gomphrena* does well in heat and tolerates drought, though it will thrive if it receives adequate moisture.

Harvest and Use Most frequently used as an everlasting, *Gomphrena* lasts indefinitely in water and is among the few flowers that last well in both water and floral foam. All of the colors combine well with many different flowers. The magenta form is stunning when used with creamy white zinnias.

You will find it necessary to harvest smaller flower buds with mature flowers; these will continue to enlarge somewhat in the arrangement, adding texture and interest. Condition the prepared stems in warm water because hot water will damage them. To use dried, hang upside down in a warm, dry, dark location. The color of the dried flower is almost as bright as that of fresh *Gomphrena.*

Gypsophila elegans (jip-SOF-i-la ay-le-GANZ) **annual baby's breath,** ○ **H**

Characteristics: Baby's breath is strongly associated with commercial florists, but it is worth including a small number of plants to provide filler for your bouquets. Annual baby's breath is a pleasant change from the *G. paniculata* 'Bristol Fairy' type typically found in flower shops. The flowers are flat, white or pale rose, and feature a single layer of five petals. Baby's breath is found in loosely branched panicles.

Cultural Information: For success over the long season, repeat sowings of seed at 2- to 3-week intervals. *Gypsophila* requires full sun and perfectly drained soils. Additions of ground agricultural limestone to the soil will aid its growth. Staking may be necessary during wet weather as "gyp" can become leggy.

Harvest and Use: Baby's breath is an excellent accent flower and gives a light airiness to bouquets. I enjoy masses of baby's breath in a vase with accents of small, colored flowers such as rose buds, bachelor's buttons and sweet Williams.

Helianthus annuus _is a vigorous addition to the sunny garden. Those not cut for inclusion in bouquets can be ripened to feed the birds._

Helianthus annuus (hee-lee-ANTH-us AN-ew-us) **sunflower,** ○ ◑ ✳ ◗ **H**

Sunflowers are a basic ingredient of many vegetable gardens where they are grown to provide food for the chickadees. Varieties such as 'Mammoth' are large flowers of the sort Van Gogh painted. They work very nicely in autumn arrangements indoors and out. However, sunflower selection need not stop at the 'Mammoth' types. A wide variety of cultivars is available in heights ranging from 2 to 12 feet. 'Color Fashion' and 'Sunburst' offer smaller versions of the favorite at a more manageable height (5 feet) and in a wider range of colors, from creamy white to yellow, gold, mahogany and brown. Many of the 3- to 5-inch flowers are made distinctive by concentric bands of contrasting color or petals accented by darker hues of the same color.

Cultural Information: Sunflowers are easy to grow in average garden soil in full sun. Sow the seed where it is to grow, thinning to a final spacing of 1 foot.

Though sunflowers tolerate drought, the quantity and quality of blooms produced will be better when they receive adequate moisture. Staking of the taller varieties should be done early as there may be a tendency for stems to be knocked over by heavy winds and late-summer rains.

Harvest and Use: Sunflowers condition nicely in hot water. Remove most of the large, coarse foliage as it taxes the stem's ability to supply water to the flower. Try combining the large forms of sunflower with other late-summer favorites. Cornstalks and other garden produce make an attractive display for the rustic porch. Smaller varieties combine well with apricot dahlias and goldenrods and look right at home in an old bronze vase.

Immortelle; see _Xeranthemum_

Kiss-me-over-the-garden-gate; see _Amaranthus_

Lace flower; see _Trachymene_

Larkspur, annual; see _Consolida_

Lathyrus odoratus (LATH-ear-us owe-DOR-ah-tus) **sweet pea,** ○ ◑ ✳ **C**

Characteristics: Sweet peas are among the truly romantic flowers of the cutting garden. They speak of a gentler time when the delicately colored blooms might be included in a nosegay or tussy-mussy. Sweet peas range from white to soft pinks, pastel lavenders and stronger shades of purple and red.

_Charm, innocence, fragrance and beauty—_Lathyrus odoratus _offers it all._

There are varieties that offer mottled flowers, bicolors and stripes. The flowers, which resemble miniature sun bonnets, are borne on short, stiff stems that branch off tendril-covered vines to 5 feet long.

Cultural Information: Sweet peas like a well-drained soil, sweetened with lime. Like other peas, the sweet pea should be planted in early spring as soon as the soil can be worked. To speed germination, soak the seed overnight to soften the seed coat. Sweet peas are a legume and do best when inoculated with a beneficial bacterium that works with the plant roots to make nitrogen available for growth. Legume Aid and Burpee Booster are two products available for this purpose. Be sure to provide a climbing support for the growing vine, be it a string trellis, teepee of poles or fencing, as unsupported sweet peas can become an unmanageable tangle.

Harvest and Use: All parts of this plant are desirable for floral design when conditioned in cool water. The gray-green foliage and twisted tendrils add charm to floral designs. Consider combining sweet peas with delicate shades of roses, forget-me-nots and blue veronicas, or keep them all to themselves for a delightfully old-fashioned bouquet.

Lisianthus; see *Eustoma*

Love-in-a-mist; see *Nigella*

Love-lies-bleeding; see *Amaranthus*

Marigold; see *Tagetes*

Marigold, pot; see *Calendula*

Mignonette; see *Reseda*

Moluccella laevis (mo-lu-KEL-la lee-VIS) **bells of Ireland,** ○ ◑ **W**

Characteristics: Green flowers are so unusual that they always receive attention. Bells of Ireland is just such an annual. The flowers are insignificant white blossoms surrounded by attractive, bright, apple green bracts (modified leaves). The bract remains showy after the flower fades. The spires of bell-shaped bracts are harvested to be used fresh or dry in bouquets.

Cultural Information: Bells of Ireland is easy to grow in a well-drained location in full sun. It is not fussy about soil but is difficult to start from seed. Refrigerate the seed for at least 5 days before soaking overnight in warm water. Press the prepared seed into the soil without covering it; the seeds need light to germinate. The bells will slowly mature through the season and in ideal circumstances reach 2 or more feet.

Moluccella laevis *is accurately described by its common name, bells of Ireland.*

Harvest and Use: Take a few moments to remove the extra leaves that appear between the bracts—I feel they detract from the form of *Moluccella*. The flowers condition well in warm water and last for 7 to 10 days as fresh cuts. To dry, hang bells of Ireland upside down in a dark, warm, dry place. Although the green will fade slightly, the spires will continue to provide interesting color and texture in dried arrangements into the winter months.

Bells of Ireland combines well with any of the "everlastings" in dried bouquets but works well with fresh flowers, too. I especially like them with some of the late-summer–blooming annuals and perennials such as *Tithonia, Aconitum,* asters and goldenrods, and there is something very pleasing about *Moluccella* with zinnias. For a change of pace, try an all-green arrangement with foliages and the flowers of the 'Envy' zinnia and 'Lime Green' nicotiana, seed heads of garlic chives, the foliage of hosta and, of course, bells of Ireland.

Mourning bride; see *Scabiosa*

Nicotiana sylvestris, N. alata (nee-KO-tee-AH-na sil-VES-tris, ah-LA-ta) **flowering tobacco, nicotiana,** ○ ◑ **W**

Characteristics: Flowering tobacco is one of the old garden standards. Like some other popular annuals, it can reseed itself and colonize in a favorable location. The flowers of *Nicotiana* are tubular, borne loosely on spikes. The colors of modern hybrids range from chartreuse to pure white, deep red and pale pink. Breeding work has encouraged varieties that are more dwarf and more basal branching. The 'Nicki Series' is 16 inches tall and provides adequate cutting stems for bouquets of average size. For an exciting statement in the vase and garden try *Nicotiana alata grandiflora* 'Fragrant Cloud', which grows to 3 feet and has fragrant, large white flowers. The *N. sylvestris* produces long stems of fragrant white flowers.

Cultural Information: Culture in the garden is easy. Seed can be sown where the plants are to grow in a well-drained, rich soil. Press seeds into the soil but do not cover, as they require light to germinate. Taller varieties may need staking. Ni-

Nicotiana alata *'Nicki Hybrid Mixed' will grow in partial shade and provide many lovely blooms for cutting.*

cotiana does well in full sun but it thrives in partial shade. In the integrated cutting garden, plant it near a terrace or bedroom window where the intoxicating fragrance can be enjoyed in the evening, when it is strongest. It may be attacked by slugs and occasionally infested with spider mites, so watch for signs of these pests.

Harvest and Use: Nicotiana can be difficult to harvest as the flowers, stems and leaves are sticky and can become so entwined they damage themselves when one tries to separate them. Harvest them individually and separate individual stems as much as possible. Give them a deep, wide bucket of warm water and spread the stems around the perimeter to avoid their tangling. Nicotiana is an exotic-looking flower for arrangements and goes well with hardy lilies, phloxes, purple coneflowers and the largest of the cosmos blossoms. In the home, place it where the fragrance can be enjoyed in the evening.

Nigella damascena (ny-JELL-a dam-a-SKAY-na) **love-in-a-mist,** ○ **W**

Characteristics: How the Victorians loved their romantic names and romantic flowers. The common name above offers a vivid picture of this excellent cut flower. *Nigella* is a small, starlike flower surrounded by a delicate spray of ferny foliage just below the flower head. Flowers range in color from pale blue-green to white, pink, blue and purple. The variety 'Persian Jewels' gives the full color range on 18-inch plants.

Cultural Information: Love-in-a-mist is a true annual, growing from seed, to flower, to fruit in short order. Once the attractive seedpods have developed, the flowers will no longer be produced. Blooming will be prolonged somewhat on plants whose flowers are harvested regularly. *Nigella* is easy to grow from seed and is likely to reseed itself if you allow a few seed heads to remain on the plant. Sow the seed every 2 to 3 months for continuous bloom from June until frost.

Harvest and Use: Harvesting love-in-a-mist is easy, and conditioning in warm water will harden cut stems nicely for use in arrangements. The seedpods can be collected and dried for use on wreaths or in dried arrangements for display throughout the autumn and winter months. The delicate colors and soft texture of *Nigella* make it easy to combine with other flowers from the garden. Choose similarly delicate flowers such as the light, snapdragon-like blooms of *Linaria*. It combines well with the smaller blooms of *Dianthus* too.

Painted tongue; see *Salpiglossis*

Pincushion flower; see *Scabiosa*

Pot marigold; see *Calendula*

Prairie gentian; see *Eustoma*

Purple umbrella; see *Trachelium*

Nigella damascena is a delightful, old-fashioned flower that produces fascinating seedpods for everlasting bouquets.

Reseda odorata (ree-SEE-da oh-do-RAH-ta) **mignonette,** ○ **C**

Characteristics: Mignonette is not an extravagant beauty that catches the eye of every passerby, but a delicate charmer with greenish blossoms that delight the sense of smell. The sweet scent of mignonette was a favorite 100 years ago, but today the plant has all but disappeared from American gardens. It grows to about 1 foot in height. The medium green leaves are topped by short spikes of dense greenish flowers often tinged with red or cream.

Cultural Information: Reseda should be sown where it is to grow in early spring. Plant in full sun and well-drained garden soil. Supplemental fertilizing will help maintain production throughout the summer, as will maintaining adequate soil moisture. A small amount included in the cutting garden is enough to provide fragrance for several bouquets all summer.

Reseda odorata is not a glamorous beauty, but will delight everyone's sense of smell with its clean, sweet aroma.

Rudbeckia hirta *is a lovely addition to any flower arrangement or late-summer garden. The flowers may be difficult to condition, but the end result is well worth the extra effort.*

Harvest and Use: Condition *Reseda* in cool water before including in bouquets. The colors are not significant enough to alter even the most delicate of color schemes very much. Use it as a filler to cover the mechanics of an arrangement while it perfumes the air.

Rudbeckia hirta (rood-BEK-ee-a her-TA) **gloriosa daisy,** ○ ◑ ☀ **W**

Zones: 3 to 9

Characteristics: Gloriosa daisies are among the most dependable summer bloomers, offering up their sunny, daisy flowers all summer long. Sometimes listed as an annual, biennial and even as a perennial, the truth of the matter is it's a free-seeding annual and will turn up in the cutting garden or integrated border season after season if allowed to go to seed. The coarse leaves and spiny stems suit this earth goddess of the

Few flowers offer the richness of color and velvety texture of Salpiglossis sinuata.

garden. Muted tones of gold, brown, yellow, burgundy and orange are typical of the varieties of this easy-to-care-for annual. Some of the more delightful specimens offer deep markings on the petals surrounding a prominent, dark brown, center cone. The variety 'Irish Eyes' has a distinctive green center that makes it a delightful accompaniment to variegated foliage.

Cultural Information: Choose a sunny place in the garden for this common roadside plant. It doesn't require an overly rich soil. *Rudbeckia* is widely available in the spring, and container-grown plants will transplant nicely. For ease in culture and cost savings, seed directly in the garden where the plants are to grow. Allow several of your favorite plants to self-sow and you will find a colony of bright, sunny blossoms each year.

Harvest and Use: Rudbeckia can be tricky to harvest and condition successfully. Cutting the stems and placing them directly into water in the garden improves chances of success, but at Mohonk we have found the florist's trick described on page 32 gives the straightest stems and the most perfect petals. Give gloriosa daisies plenty of room in the conditioning container; the blooms are up to 5 inches across, and the petals are easily damaged. Once turgid after conditioning, the flowers are long lasting and will grace a vase of fresh water for more than a week.

Arranging with gloriosa daisies is fun, as their bright colors and sturdy, no-nonsense look are always uplifting. Com-

bine them with other rugged members of the cutting garden such as yarrow and blanketflower, add some down-home roadside selections such as grass heads and sedges, and you'll have the quintessential all-American bouquet! What better way to accent a picnic table for a summer barbecue?

Sage, garden; see *Salvia*

Salpiglossis (sal-pi-GLOSS-iss sin-yew-AH-ta) **velvet flower, painted tongue,** ○ ◑ ☀ **S,W**

Characteristics: This petunia relative is a delightful addition to the cutting garden where summers are cool. The intensely colored flowers in shades of gold, blue, purple, maroon and yellow are rich additions to almost any flower arrangement. The variety 'Casino' is an 18- to 24-inch annual that features the full mix of colors, many with brightly streaked and veined throats.

Cultural Information: Salpiglossis can be sown directly in the garden, successfully started indoors or purchased from the nursery. Plant in a rich, light, well-drained soil in full sun to partial shade. Those planted in shade tend to be a little taller, but where summer heat is a problem, light shade will make for better success.

Harvest and Use: Cut *Salpiglossis* carefully, for like their cousin nicotiana, *Salpiglossis* clings to itself. Always cut them last, and carefully arrange them on top of other flowers in the cutting basket; try to keep them away from each other.

Painted tongue's velvety texture and rich colors give it a commanding presence in the vase. Combine it with other strong colors such as cherry red snapdragon or blue *Salvia*, or choose a more subtle cast of players with the delicate shadings of *Digitalis* and the gray foliage of *Artemisia*.

Salvia (sal-VEE-a) **garden sage**, ○ **W**

Zones: 4 to 9

Characteristics: The garden sages, a marvelous group, may be perennial or annual. The most common form, *Salvia splendens,* scarlet sage, is an old-fashioned favorite in the garden but perhaps should no longer be referred to as the scarlet sage. *S. splendens* comes in a variety of sizes and colors, including purple, rose, coral and white. The flowers of this member of the mint family are tubular and relatively short lived. The calyx, a long-lasting, brightly colored tube, remains showy long after the actual flower has faded. This is a warm-weather garden grower.

Salvia farinacea, mealycup sage, offers one of the best blues for the cutting garden and integrated border. This delightful native American provides an excellent source of true blue spikes for arrangements. The variety 'Argent' (or 'White Porcelain') is a silvery white companion. The 6- to 8-inch flower spikes top 8- to 10-inch stems. Consider 'Blue Bedder', which grows to about 30 inches, or for a shorter plant (18 inches), 'Victoria'. *S. farinacea* and *S. splendens* are perennials in warmer climates. In the Northeast it is best to treat them both as annuals.

Salvia horminum, Joseph's coat, is a delightful, small, textured sage and a true annual, completing its life cycle in 1 year. It may also be called the clary sage, which is a misnomer (clary sage is *S. sclarea*). The colorful bracts in pale pink, white or blue will provide a copious supply of color for fresh-cut or dried bouquets. Sow the seed where it is to grow. Joseph's coat will frequently reseed itself and return to the garden for many seasons.

Salvia patens, the gentian sage, is a lesser-known cousin of the other annual and tender perennial sages. This salvia is perhaps one of the boldest of blue flowers. Although the flowers are not as prolific as the other sages, the clear azure blue of gentian sage will bring a bright, bold accent to the garden.

Cultural Information: Give the sage a hot, sunny spot in the garden, and you will be happy with the profusion of blooms suitable for fresh and dry use. *Salvia* varieties are available at local greenhouses each spring; look for varieties that will be tall enough to provide good length in cutting stems. Although *Salvia* tolerates poor soils and drought, give it a rich soil with plenty of organic matter and adequate moisture to see it thrive. *S. horminum* will reseed and colonize in the garden, providing years of cutting materials from one sowing.

Harvest and Use: Floral combinations are unlimited with the blues of *S. horminum, S. farinacea* and *S. patens.* Combina- tions with summer-blooming annuals such as marigolds and zinnias work well, as do such elegant flowers as lilies and roses. The upright flower spikes are the ideal counterpoint to the rounded flower forms like those of zinnias. The brilliant scarlet sage will become a delightful accent for marigolds in late summer or early autumn.

Scabiosa atropurpurea
(skāb-ee-O-sa ah-tro-pur-PEWR-ee-a) **pincushion flower, mourning bride**, ○ **W**

Characteristics: The reaction to *Scabiosa* is always the same: "Why does such a pretty flower have such an unpleasant name?" *Scabiosa* is an arrestingly beautiful flower. Its simplicity is deceiving. The fully double, rounded heads are composed of intricate series of individual blooms in deep red, blue, white and every pastel shade in between. Light-colored stamens extend above the petals of the flowers like pins from a pincushion, hence one of its common names. Plants may reach 3 feet in height, and individual flower stems average 1 or more feet, making them long-lasting favorites of the home flower arranger.

Cultural Information: Scabiosa is easy to grow in a well-drained, rich garden soil. Start plants indoors or sow seed directly in May for good cut-flower production from August through a killing frost. Few pests bother the pincushion flower. Look for the 'Giant Imperial' variety for cutting. Offering a superior mix of colors, it behaves nicely in the garden and rarely needs staking.

The garden sages (Salvia *spp.) will provide many flowers for cutting and drying. Blue salvia (*S. farinacea*) is among the best of all the blue flowers for cutting.*

Scabiosa atropurpurea *has wonderful, mounded flowers in a rich range of colors. The wiry stems support the flowers well in arrangements.*

The Signet Marigolds (Tagetes signata 'Pumila') will delight you. These tiny blossoms are borne in sprays with fernlike foliage.

Harvest and Use: Cutting *Scabiosa* is easy as the foliage is mostly basal. Properly conditioned in warm water, it isn't unusual for pincushion flowers to last as long as 2 weeks. The range of colors represented in *Scabiosa* makes the blossoms easy to use with many other garden flowers. August and September are rich months in the cutting garden, with abundant selections and combinations from which to choose. Try the deep red, almost black *Scabiosa* with garden phlox and globe amaranth for an intriguing contrast of forms and textures. The pastel shades are well offset by the deep blue-violet hues of *Aconitum*, and any of them will work well with lisianthuses which run in a similar color range and will harmonize well in an analogous color scheme.

Snapdragon; see ***Antirrhinum***

Snow-on-the-mountain; see ***Euphorbia***

Sunflower; see ***Helianthus***

Marigolds, Tagetes erecta, *are some of the most rewarding flowers for the cutting garden: they are easy to grow and inexpensive and their garden performance is matched by their beauty in the vase.*

Sweet pea; see ***Lathyrus***

Sweet William; see ***Dianthus***

Tagetes (ta-GAY-teez) marigold, ○ ◗ ✳ **W**

Characteristics: The common marigold, an excellent cut flower, is probably not used as much as it should be. Perhaps this is because it is often one of the first plants many of us grow, and we associate it with our unsophisticated beginnings. It's true some people are repelled by the pungent foliage. I'm one of those people who takes comfort in that familiar smell. But for those who are hesitant, many of today's marigolds have a less pungent foliage than their ancestors, and some varieties have odorless foliage.

Cultural Information: Marigolds are Mexican natives and thrive in a hot, dry garden environment in well-drained soil. Purchase plants from the nursery in spring or seed them where they are to grow in the sunny garden. Like many annuals, marigolds will tolerate drought but produce more cuttable stems when grown in well-prepared, fertile soil with adequate moisture. Their ease in culture, bold color and long-lasting vase life make them ideal subjects for the cutting garden.

Harvest and Use: Tagetes is easily harvested and conditioned. Cleaned stems can be placed in warm water to harden, for use in fresh water or floral foam. They last equally well in water and floral foam. During the cooler autumn months, harvest marigolds in the warmer part of the day; they are better able to absorb water when warm.

Three species of *Tagetes* are typically available as seedlings: *T. erecta* (the African marigold), *T. patula* (the French marigold) and *T. signata pumila* (the signet marigold). The names are ironic, as all marigolds are native Americans. The African marigold is also called the American marigold or hedge marigold. These are the tallest of the marigolds, growing to 3 or more feet with flowers to 4 inches across. I like using the big, bold, brassy African marigold with the bright red *Salvia* 'Early Bonfire' for a neon announcement that summer is over!

The French marigolds are dwarfs, with heights of 6 to 12 inches. Free flowering, French marigold blooms are 1 inch across and may be single, fully double, anenome-flowered or crested in form. These are delightful garden subjects but frequently don't provide adequate stem length to make them worthwhile in the cutting garden.

The African and French marigolds have been crossed and are called triploid, mule or Afro-French marigolds. Many of these are only 12 to 14 inches high, bearing large flowers similar to those of the African types. Their short stems are difficult to use in flower designs.

To me the most delightful and useful of the marigolds is the signet marigold. These 12- to 14-inch plants produce the smallest of the marigold blooms at ½ inch across. The single blossoms are borne in profusion atop ferny foliage that has a distinctly lemony fragrance. This marigold produces 8- to 10-inch stems of flower sprays that add delightful texture when used as filler in arrangements. The variety 'Lemon Gem' is clean medium yellow. Combine it with *Lisianthus* 'Yodel Blue' or with *Gomphrena globosa* 'Strawberry Fields'. The individual blossoms of 'Lemon Gem' can be added (if they have not been sprayed) to a tossed salad for extra color and a unique, pungent flavor.

Tobacco, flowering; see *Nicotiana*

Trachelium caeruleum
(tray-KEEL-ee-um   see-RU-lee-um)
blue throatwort, purple umbrella, ○ W
Characteristics: Trachelium, a tender perennial, will overwinter in the South. It forms dense heads of smoky, deep purple flowers borne on tough, wiry stems. The stems in and of themselves are of interest and appear almost black. The panicles of flowers are useful in bouquets where their distinctive form, texture and faint fragrance complement almost any other flower types.
Cultural Information: Trachelium seeds are tiny and should be started indoors on a sunny windowsill 6 to 8 weeks before the last spring frost. They tolerate cool temperatures and will bloom from midsummer until frost when planted in a sunny location.
Harvest and Use: Trachelium is so stiff you can almost use it

without conditioning. The flowers will last for 1 month or longer in arrangements and show no preference to either water or floral foam. Combine *Trachelium* 'Purple Umbrella' with *Tithonia*, the Mexican sunflower, or the orange zinnia for a bright contrast in colors. Or, use them with *Delphinium*, dahlias or lilies for a more elegant effect. The white form ('White Umbrella') is available but doesn't appeal to me, as the white blossoms appear almost dirty against the dark stems.

Trachymene coerulea
(tra-kee-MAY-nee   ko-ROO-lee-ah)
blue lace flower, ○ ✳ W
Characteristics: The Victorians loved these umbels of pale blue, fragrant flowers. This little-known, easy-to-grow annual is best grown in the cutting garden as plants may become scrappy looking as the season progresses. These plants produce dozens of blooms and resemble pale blue Queen Anne's lace. Flower production may slow down during the hot summer months if night temperatures exceed 70 degrees Fahrenheit.
Cultural Information: Sow the seeds where they are to grow about the time of the last spring frost. The plants will grow to a height of 18 inches and will spread to 1 or more feet. Space seedlings 8 to 10 inches apart for best flower production. *Trachymene* doesn't like to dry out, so water well during drought. Regular harvesting will help promote flower production.
Harvest and Use: Cut, stripped of its light green, deeply lobed

foliage, and conditioned in warm water, *Trachymene* is one of the longest-lasting cut flowers. Try combining it with other flowers of delicate hue such as sweet peas, pale pink lisianthuses and pink *Salvia horminum*, or try the pale yellow of *Calendula*, deep green foliage of *Arborvitae*, and a stronger blue as of larkspurs. This blossom becomes "something blue" in wedding bouquets, especially lovely when mixed with creamy white roses and baby's breath.

Umbrella, purple; see *Trachelium*

Trachelium caeruleum has wiry stems supporting deep purple-blue flowers borne in flat-top clusters. The flowers, though small, create a wonderfully hazy look in arrangements.

Try old-fashioned Trachymene *in combination with other pastel flowers for a delicate, feminine bouquet.*

Verbena bonariensis *often reseeds and colonizes in the garden. It is best to plant this vigorous, 4-foot-tall grower in the background.*

Grow Xeranthemum annuum *for fresh or dry use in the sunny garden.*

Zinnias are never out of style.

Velvet flower; see *Salpiglossis*

Verbena bonariensis

(ver-BEE-na bon-AR-ee-EN-sis) **verbena,** ○ ◉ ✳ **W**

Characteristics: There are many verbenas available from seed catalogs for growing in sunny spots of the garden, but none will provide the stem length and garden show of *Verbena bonariensis*. *V. bonariensis* reaches 4 to 5 feet, and its strong, stiff, upright stems support the dense clusters of rosy purple flowers without staking.

Cultural Information: Seed directly into the garden in full sun and thin to 12 inches apart. The young plants will appear leggy and spare when young, but a cluster of six to eight plants will quickly put on a display of note. Allow a few blossoms to ripen at the end of the season as the plant will reseed and a natural-looking colony will develop. In the garden combine *V. bonariensis* with cosmos, cleome and *Artemisia ludoviciana* 'Silver King' for a free-flowing, long-flowering display of self-sufficient plants.

Harvest and Use: Verbena is easy to condition and will last for 7 to 10 days in water. Use warm water to condition the stems, which require little or no stripping of foliage. In the vase, combine it with some of its garden friends, cosmos and the silvery foliage of *Artemisia*. The color will glow among pink and lavender flowers of any type.

Xeranthemum annuum

(ze-RAN-the-mum an-NEW-um) **immortelle,** ○ ✳ ◉ **W**

Characteristics: Frequently listed among everlastings, immortelle is an easily grown, trouble-free flower for use in fresh and dried bouquets. These composite flowers are on 3-foot plants characterized by white, softly furred leaves and stems. The plants will bear blossoms of pale pink, white, rose and lilac in single and double forms. Individual blossoms are small (1¼ inches in diameter), but the plants produce generous amounts suitable for fresh and dried use as well as plenty left over for garden display.

Cultural Information: Like so many of the everlastings, *Xeranthemum* requires full sun in average, well-drained garden soil. It can be started indoors in a sunny, warm location in March for transplanting into the garden after all danger of frost. Seed it directly out of doors after danger of frost for late-summer bloom.

Harvest and Use: Immortelle combines well with other everlastings such as *Gomphrena* and *Helichrysum* in either fresh or dried form. However, the soft, grayish white stems and shiny flowers mix best with flowers of more satiny texture. Try combining it with *Salpiglossis* or *Ageratum*. I like the colors and textures mixed with the deep red foliage of *Ocimum basilicum* 'Purple Ruffles' (purple basil) or *Perilla,* too.

Zinnia elegans (zin-EE-ah EL-e-ganz) **zinnia,** ○ **W**

Characteristics: Zinnias are like old friends: They are comfortable to be around, and though undemanding, they do much to enrich our lives. Zinnias are true summer annuals, basking in bright sun and hot days. Zinnia colors are strong, and flowers make a bold statement in form and colors. The petals have an unusual satiny quality and seem to shine as if coated with reflective dust. This gives the zinnia blossom an inner light. Two of the best varieties for cutting are 'Cut and Come Again', with 1½-inch blooms, and 'State Fair', with blossoms up to 3 inches across. These two varieties complement each other well, with flowers that range from creamy white to soft pink, hot pink, magenta and deep rose to bright red. Interspersed are plants producing flowers from the palest yellow to deep gold and clear orange to bronze. Both grow on sturdy plants to 36 inches. *Zinnia* 'Envy' is a green variety that may have some people looking askance, but when combined with the whites of snapdragons, nicotianas, bells of Ireland and the foliage of snow-on-the-mountain, the effect is remarkably cool and elegant.

Cultural Information: Zinnias can be seeded directly in the garden or purchased as seedlings in spring. Wait until the soil has warmed and all danger of frost is past before planting. Zinnias are prone to powdery mildew in late summer and will benefit from a full-sun location with plenty of room around them for good air movement. If possible, avoid watering with overhead sprinklers, as this promotes conditions favorable to the disease. 'State Fair' may need staking, but the smaller-flowered 'Cut and Come Again' will do very nicely on its own. *Harvest and Use:* Zinnias are delightfully easy to cut for use in flower arrangements. Like many annuals, zinnias produce more and better blooms as the season progresses; don't be afraid to cut heavily. The leaves are attached tightly to the stem and care must be used in removing them as the stems are easily bent. Zinnia blooms should be cut in the warmer part of the day during the cool autumn months as they will not condition well when stems are cold. Condition zinnias in warm, not hot, water; even though the plants thrive in summer heat, the flower stems can be damaged by excessive heat.

Zinnias are among the most versatile of all the cutting flowers. They will last for 1 or more weeks in water, and are in bloom for such a long period in the garden that you will be able to create different combinations from June through October. Try deep rose zinnias with creamy white *Astilbe* in June, hot pink and magenta zinnias with *Liatris* in July, yellow zinnias with yellow lilies and ferns in August, and greet autumn with orange and bronze zinnias with *Gaillardia* and gloriosa daisies in September.

PERENNIALS

Achillea (ah-KEEL-ee-a) **yarrow**, ○ ◗ **H**
Zones: 3 to 8
Characteristics: The yarrows are easy additions to the cutting garden, where they perform well in hot, sunny, dry conditions and even in poorer soils. Yarrows are native Americans and bring with them an inbred hardiness and disease resistance. Several species are worth including in the cutting garden, many producing blooms suitable for both fresh and dry use.

Achillea × 'Coronation Gold' is a standard in the perennial border and should be planted in the cutting garden for its profuse display of quality flowers. The stems of the brilliant golden yellow flower heads reach 3 feet, giving them the height needed for even the largest floral designs. Individual heads may be as much as 3 inches across, easy to use in almost any bouquet. Like that of many *Achillea* varieties the foliage of *A.* × 'Coronation Gold' is mostly basal, finely serrated and soft gray-green.

A. filipendulina is the fernleaf yarrow. It is the tallest of the yarrows, topping out at close to 5 feet. The flower heads are a strong golden yellow and reach 4 to 5 inches across. The gray-green foliage can reach 10 inches long and makes a suitable cut green when harvested and conditioned in warm water.

A. millefolium, common yarrow, offers several suitable cutting varieties. Try 'Cerise Queen', 'Rubra' or 'Rosea' for their flower heads in pinks and reds borne atop 2- to 2½-foot stems. 'Summer Pastels' is a new introduction, named an All-America Selection winner. The softly muted pinks, cream, buff and pale yellow flowers offer a soft, muted palette.

Cultural Information: Yarrow is one of the easiest plants to cultivate. Purchase named varieties from a reliable nursery or mail-order catalog in spring. Plant them in a well-dug garden site in full sun; take care to avoid creating an overrich soil because lush growth will be weak and floppy, requiring

Achillea *'Summer Pastels' from the Mohonk Gardens. The delicate shading of rose, yellow, blush and creamy white blend well in the garden and the vase.*

Aconitum *is a great cutting garden perennial. The blue cowls borne on spikes up to 4 feet tall give it the common name monkshood.*

Aquilegia *spp. will delight the gardener in partial shade. Try combining columbine with tulips or bleeding heart and bring spring indoors in a vase.*

staking. *A. millefolium* varieties become weedy in the garden; don't hesitate to divide them regularly to avoid overcrowding and reduce production. Yarrow is easily grown from seed and will flower the first year. Though yarrows tolerate drought when established, maintain adequate soil moisture during dry periods to promote high-quality flowers and healthy plants.

Harvest and Use: The yarrows offer coarse texture for the garden and vase, yet there is something very rich looking about the brilliant yellow heads, especially of *A. filipendulina* 'Gold Plate'. Cut and condition overnight in hot water for longest-lasting blooms in either fresh water or floral foam.

I like combining the yellow yarrows with strong foliages such as hosta which contrast nicely in texture. In a vase with deep purple *Delphinium* and *Astilbe*, yarrow is a standout. When dried, the heads can be cut from their stems and used in wreaths, where they'll hold their color long into the season.

Aconitum (ah-KO-ny-tum)
monkshood, ○ ◐ ✳ H
Zones: 5 to 8
Characteristics: Monkshood is a reliable alternative to *Delphinium* for the late-summer and early-fall border and cutting garden. The individual flowers in deep, rich blues and purples look like the cowled hoods worn by the brothers in the monastery, hence the name "monkshood."

There are actually several colors available in the genus

Aconitum: Choose *A.* × *bicolor* for distinctive white flowers edged in blue; *A. napellus* 'Albus' for white; and for yellow or creamy white flowers, grow *A. vulparia*. In my estimation, the finest of form and color is the azure monkshood (*A. carmichaelii*), which grows to 4 feet. The flowers of azure monkshood, a deep purple-blue, are borne on long, tapering spikes.

Cultural Information: Aconitum prefers cool climates and rich garden soils that receive regular applications of organic matter and fertilizer. Purchase plants from a local nursery or buy the bare-root plants sold through many reputable mail-order houses. Soak the roots of bareroot plants overnight in warm water before planting for the best results.

Planted in light shade, *Aconitum* thrives for many years without being divided. A light, organic mulch will help conserve moisture and keep roots cool through the hot summer months.

Harvest and Use: Cut stems should be conditioned in hot water. In an arrangement, monkshood is happiest in plenty of water. Combine monkshood with yarrows, China asters, phloxes and hardy asters.

Aquilegia (ak-will-EE-jee-a)
columbine, ◐ ○ ● ✳ C
Zones: 4 to 8
Characteristics: Columbines are old-fashioned favorites that surely graced grandmother's garden as they grace our own in May and June. The multicolored, nodding blossoms are held above light green foliage

reminiscent of maidenhair ferns. The intricate blossoms appear to be fragile, which belies the lasting quality they possess. Brightly colored sepals that may form elongated spurs add an exotic flair to the flowers in blues, pinks, yellows, red and white. The foliage can be cut for inclusion in flower arrangements, as can the seed heads, which are four-parted, upright cylindrical chambers. Columbines grow to 3 feet, depending on site and variety.

Try growing *A. caerulea* for its lovely blue and white flowers. The various varieties of *A.* × *hybrida* offer the largest assortment of colors and flower types. 'Nora Barlow' is a double flower with pink, red, green and white tones. The McKana Giant hybrids are among the largest flowered of all the varieties, with a full artist's palette of colors. 'Snow Queen' is pure white and very elegant.

Cultural Information: Columbines will grow in full sun, but do even better in partial shade as it provides a cooler environment. They require a perfectly drained soil to avoid root rot, which makes columbines relatively short-lived perennials.

The plants are easily grown from seed and may resist transplanting because of their tap root. Be prepared for them to reseed and form colonies. Hybrid columbines will generally not come true from seed collected in the garden, and an interesting selection may be found in subsequent generations, but don't be surprised if the color assortment and exotic spurs both start to disappear. Consider reseeding columbine every other year or so to keep a fresh supply of a wide range of colors and form. Columbine will occasionally suffer from leaf miners, which feed between the upper and lower leaf surfaces, leaving irregular trails to mar the foliage.

Harvest and Use: Harvest back to the crown of the plant to get the longest stems possible. Columbines should be conditioned in cool water, which firms them nicely without hastening their demise. Fresh columbines last in the vase for 5 to 7 days. Combine columbines with other spring-flowering favorites. Try forget-me-nots, bleeding hearts, daffodils and tulips for a light-hearted, romantic garden bouquet.

Artemisia (ar-tay-MIS-ee-a) wormwood, mugwort, ○ ◑ ✳ H

Zones: 5 to 8

Characteristics: Artemisia is a native American and always a valued addition to the landscape and the vase. Typically, the wormwoods are grown for their finely cut, silvery foliage. Wormwood is a long-lived addition to the garden and easy to care for, with few pests or diseases.

Artemisia ludoviciana albula is the full Latin name for two of the best varieties for cutting and drying. 'Silver King' is a 3-foot plant, and 'Silver Queen' is a shorter relative; they produce large amounts of silvery white foliage.

Cultural Information: Plant the nursery-grown or bareroot plants in the garden in a well-drained soil in full sun. The soil should not be too rich, as this encour-

ages legginess and weak stems that may require staking.

Harvest and Use: Harvest in late morning after the dew has dried, and condition the stems in hot water. If the foliage is wetted, it will appear to be green until it dries to a silvery white again. The yellow blossoms that form in June do not become a significant element of any display. I like to combine the silvery foliage of *Artemisia* with strong colors of the richest hues. *Celosia* and *Salvia* combine well with *Artemisia,* as do bold, red dahlias. Wormwood combines well with other foliage, and it is wonderful to see what happens when burgundy foliage is combined with silver. Pure white flowers of any species combine elegantly with *Artemisia.*

Aster (A-ster) **Michaelmas daisy,** ○ ◑ H

Zones: 3–8

Characteristics: Asters are among the best of the late-summer perennials for the cutting garden. They are long lasting in water and offer a color range to please even the most jaded. Several varieties provide suitable cuts. *Aster × frikartii* is one of the best, with an unparalleled season of bloom; these plants produce a large number of pale lavender-blue flowers singly at the ends of stems. *A. novae-angliae,* the New England aster, produces beautiful pink to lilac, daisylike flowers on plants that may grow 4 to 5 feet tall. *A. novi-belgi,* the New York aster, is not nearly as tall as its New England cousin but produces flowers that range from white to navy blue on

plants to 3 feet. Both the New York and the New England aster are commonly found along roadsides and in waste places and meadows throughout the Northeast. The colors range from grayish white to deep blue, and although the flowers are usually quite small in the wild, you may find some that are showy and worthy of cutting.

Cultural Information: The taller asters may require staking, as they are prone to damage from the wind and heavy rains that may plague the late-summer garden. Give asters plenty of space in the border or cutting garden as they may mildew during the dog days of summer when humidity abounds and air sits stagnant. Dividing clumps of asters regularly is beneficial, not only to keep plants rejuvenated but to refresh the soil and space the plants out for better growth and development. Asters may be grown from seed, but the best results usually are obtained from container-grown or bareroot specimens purchased for spring planting.

Choose a rich garden site in full sun or light shade. Asters will frequently tolerate poor soils, but the plant height and flower size may suffer. Once established, hardy garden asters are likely to overrun the garden, and despite their loveliness they should be rogued out like any other weed. I always enjoy garden flowers that have a little spunk and offer "extras" to any gardening neighbor willing to take some off my hands.

Harvest and Use: Asters are easy to harvest and condition. The foliage, borne along the

The silvery-grey foliage of Artemisia ludoviciana 'Silver King' *performs well in the sunny garden even in poor soils. Use it in arrangements either fresh or dried. Wormwood's grey foliage will combine well with a large variety of strong-colored flowers and foliages.*

Asters can often be found growing along the roadsides or in waste places. The improved varieties of Aster × frikartii *come in shades of blue, violet, rose, pink and white.*

length of the flower stem, easily strips off for additions to the compost pile. The flowers firm up very nicely in warm to hot water. Asters last well in floral foam but, like other flowers, really do best in clean water. Asters, with their yellow centers and petals in shades of blue and violet, combine well with many garden flowers. Try large masses of goldenrod with equally large masses of *A. novibelgi* 'Sailor Boy' for a delightfully wild-looking summer bouquet. Or combine white nicotianas with a mixture of asters in blue, pink and violet for a visual and fragrant sensation.

Astilbe (a-STIL-bee) **false spirea,** ◐ ○ ✳ **H**

Zones: 4 to 8
Characteristics: With frosty spires of delicate white or pink blooms, or in bold red or maroon, *Astilbe* is a graceful garden perennial that excels in fresh flower arrangements and dried bouquets. *Astilbe* ranges in height from 1 to 4 feet and will happily occupy a moist location in the shady garden. The ferny, dark green foliage is excellent in the garden and can be harvested for use in a vase of fresh-cut flowers. By carefully selecting varieties, you can have *Astilbe* in bloom from June into September.

Astilbe is a charming perennial for partial shade and woodsy soils rich in organic matter. The delicate spires of frothy blooms can be cut. Astilbe *foliage is a natural addition to any* astilbe *bouquet.*

Cultural Information: Astilbe is best purchased from the nursery or through a reputable mail-order house; bareroot plants should be planted in spring. As with any bareroot perennial, soak the plants overnight in warm water before planting. *Astilbe* requires soil deeply prepared with plenty of organic matter such as compost, leaf mold or well-rotted manure. A protected, partially shady site is ideal for these garden favorites that don't like extreme heat. Divide *Astilbe* every three years or so, to allow you to enrich the soil. They will reward you with larger blooms and more of them.
Harvest and Use: Harvest while the plants are quite young. If you wait until all of the flowers have opened on these graceful spires, they will shatter and not last in water. White blooms may turn brown as they fade. *Astilbe* has little foliage on the strong, wiry stems. Condition cut spires overnight in hot water before arranging them in a deep vase with a large water reservoir. I love to design with astilbes in all of their colors and will combine them with lilies, delphiniums, roses, snapdragons, *Allium* and almost any other flower. Their natural beauty and texture complement so many other flowers. Remember to save some for drying. In the integrated garden you will be hard-pressed to leave some behind for garden display.

Baby's breath, hardy; see *Gypsophila*

Bee balm; see *Monarda*

The genus Campanula *is a large one with many cultivars. The peach-leafed bellflower offers a tall spire of bell like flowers in pristine white or deep blue.*

Bellflower; see *Campanula*

Bergamot; see *Monarda*

Blanketflower; see *Gaillardia*

Campanula (kam-PAN-new-la) **bellflower,** ○ ◐ ● **H**

Zones: 3 to 7
Characteristics: The bellflowers are a large group of herbaceous biennials and perennials, many of which are suitable for cutting. Perhaps one of the best for cutting is *Campanula persicifolia*, the peach-leafed bellflower, which has long been a popular cut flower in Europe and for several years a Dutch import to the United States for the florist trade. The peach-leafed bellflower is available in shades of blue and pure white.
Cultural Information: C. persicifolia is an easy-to-grow peren-

nial that will adapt to conditions from full sun to shade. Plant seed in late spring in the nursery row, and transplant in August where they are to bloom the following spring. Nursery-grown plants are also available. Most varieties grow to about 3 feet and should be spaced at about 12 inches in rich garden loam. Irrigate regularly during the blooming period from late June through July. Plants can be divided easily once established to propagate new plants and improve soil fertility.

Harvest and Use: These wonderfully stately spires are superb companions for peonies, and complement lilies in both color and form. Combine them with many of the spring-blooming shrubs such as rhododendron and beautybush. The foliage is mostly basal and conditioning in hot water is recommended. Once conditioned, bellflowers will last for 10 to 14 days in water.

Chrysanthemum (kris-ANTH-em-um) **shasta daisy, painted daisy, hardy garden chrysanthemum,** ○ ◑ ✳ **S,W**

Zones: 5 to 9
Characteristics: Chrysanthemum is a large genus of composite flowers, many of which are suitable for cutting. *C.* × *superbum* is one of the best, the shasta daisy. These are the large white "daisy" daisies, with yellow centers and white petals that are the essence of early summer and purity. Several varieties are available for cutting. Shasta 'Alaska' is a 2-inch daisy on 2-foot stems; it

is manageable in bouquets and easily conditioned. Shasta 'Majestic' is one of the largest, with flowers almost 6 inches across on 2-foot plants. These may be "majestic," but they are not easily conditioned or used in flower bouquets, because the large flowers are awkwardly out of proportion to their stem length.

The painted daisy, *C. coccineum,* is a yellow-centered flower in shades of pink and crimson. The plants are typically straight stemmed with soft, ferny foliage. 'Robinson's Pink' and 'Robinson's Carmine' are two named varieties suitable for cutting.

Hardy garden chrysanthemums, or "mums," are the delight of the autumn garden. *C.* × *morifolium* is a diverse group of plants that includes single, daisylike varieties and fully double forms, in colors ranging from white to maroon and some that are truly bronze. These garden favorites, sold by the roadsides each autumn, are delightful late-summer additions of color to porches and planting beds. The large assortment of flower types, colors and season of bloom make this an ideal addition to the cutting garden. Choose several varieties for a full range of characteristics.

Cultural Information: Shasta daisies are easily grown from root divisions, seed or plants bought from the nursery or mail-order house. They are gregarious in the garden and multiply, sometimes becoming a nuisance. Seed mixes of painted daisy are available, but selected plants should be chosen from the mix as some

Daisies are the very essence of innocence and summer fun. Chrysanthemum maximum *are easy to grow and harvest for use in flower bouquets.*

flowers will be imperfect in form and unsuitable for use in design. Once you have selected the flowers and colors suited to your needs, discard the rest and propagate your selections by division.

For best results with hardy mums in the cutting garden, purchase young rooted cuttings or bareroot plants in spring. Division of existing garden plants each spring will give you an endless supply of vigorous plant stock for the cutting garden. The culture will vary with their use. In the ornamental garden you may want to pinch new growth back every few weeks until the Fourth of July; flower buds will follow. Pinching produces the well-rounded, bushy plants we have come to recognize as the hardy garden mum. For cutting, however, we don't want to pinch out new growth and encourage densely branched plants. We want to encourage good stem length. Toward the end of the season, the mum will naturally branch out and you will have a spray of blossoms suitable for cutting and use in bouquets.

Chrysanthemums are not fussy about soil but should be grown in full sun or, at most, very light shade. A well-prepared, rich soil will give you longer stems for cutting. Fall-flowering mums should be divided each spring and will give you a large number of young, vigorous shoots to plant; discard the woody stems. Divide shastas and painted daisies after they bloom each year in midsummer. Take that opportunity to improve the soil with plenty of compost or well-rotted manure. Staking may be necessary in very fertile soils or in shade to keep the stems off of the ground.

Harvest and Use: Chrysanthemums are easy to condition and use. For shastas the florist's cardboard trick described on page 32 will keep the stems

Convallaria majalis *will form a dense groundcover in moist, shady areas and provide generous numbers of stems with which to fill delicate vases. Their fragrance and simple beauty need no accompaniment.*

straight and allow the flower petals to become turgid in a flat plane. Combine shastas with astilbes, larkspurs or *Campanula*. The pinks and reds of the painted daisies combine nicely with mock orange and white *Salvia horminum*. Autumn mums are fine all by themselves, but when combined with other late-summer and fall bloomers such as asters, sunflowers and the heads of ornamental grasses or roadside weeds, they become the official welcoming committee for the glories of autumn.

Columbine; see *Aquilegia*

Coneflower, purple; see *Echinacea*

Convallaria majalis (kon-val-AIR-ee-a may-JALL-iss) **lily of the valley,** ◑ ● C
Zones: 3 to 9
Characteristics: Lily of the valley makes a wonderful groundcover for the shadiest places in the integrated cutting garden. In the right location it forms a dense groundcover with fragrant white blossoms that sweeten the garden each June. The flowers are small, white bells on delicately arching stems and may reach only 6 inches in height. There are several varieties available, including a pink form and a double form, but quite frankly, only the species is worth growing.
Cultural Information: Lily of the valley requires a rich, well-drained soil with plenty of moisture. Annual topdressings of peat moss or well-rotted manure will benefit this garden beauty. Basically trouble free,

foliage of *Convallaria* will become pale and shabby looking if it dries out or is overcrowded. Additional plants are propagated through division of established clumps in early spring. Both the roots and the orange-red globular fruits are poisonous if ingested.
Harvest and Use: The best way to harvest lily of the valley is to grasp the stem close to where it emerges from the foliage and gently tug it straight up. This will maximize the stem length and leave the plants looking tidy. Recut the stems with sharp snips or shears before conditioning in cool water. When picking, cut a few leaves to complement the flowers, as the long, parallel-veined leaves look better with lily of the valley than any other foliage. *Convallaria* is best used alone or with other small-scale, spring-flowering plants such as grape hyacinths, violets and forget-me-nots.

Coralbells; see *Heuchera*

Coreopsis (ko-ree-OP-sis gran-di-FLO-ra) **lance coreopsis, tickseed,** ○ ◑ ◐ ✳ W
Zones: 3 to 9
Characteristics: Coreopsis is a native American plant that produces a profusion of golden yellow blossoms from June through the fall months. The basal foliage is composed of dark green, lance-shaped foliage; the flower heads are produced on strong, straight, leafless stems. The variety 'Early Sunrise' will bloom the first year from seed and is ideal for cutting.

Coreopsis lanceolata *with black-eyed Susan and gray lamb's ear fill this perennial border with more than enough flowers. A few won't be missed when cut and brought indoors for enjoyment at the dining table.*

Coreopsis grandiflora *'Early Sunrise' is a perennial that is easily grown from seed and will bloom the first year.*

Cultural Information: Coreopsis is an easy-to-grow perennial that will thrive in deep, well-drained soils enriched with organic matter in hot, sunny locations. Sow the seed where they are to grow and thin to 8 inches apart. Coreopsis needs no staking and welcomes supplemental watering during periods of dry weather.

Harvest and Use: Harvesting flowers is the key to a continuous display in the garden, and the flowers will last for 1 or more weeks in an arrangement.

When coreopsis is conditioned and turgid, combine it with blue larkspurs, lavenders or blue *Salvia* for the natural complement of yellow and blue, or combine it with bronze snapdragons, *Gaillardia* and mahogany sunflowers or gloriosa daisies for a celebration of earth tones.

Daisy, painted; see ***Chrysanthemum***

Daisy, shasta; see ***Chrysanthemum***

Delphinium elatum hybrids (dell-FIN-ee-um ee-LAY-tum) delphinium, ○ ◐ ✳H

Zones: 3 to 8

Characteristics: No garden should be without delphiniums, and no one who seriously wants to produce an exciting spring bouquet can pass them up. Delphiniums are tall, stately garden specimens, demanding of the site and gardener alike. The elegant spikes in shades ranging from the deepest purple to the palest blue and pure white are frequently accented with white or black centers, known as "bees."

Many strains of excellent garden delphiniums are available. The 'Blackmore and Langdon Strain' is exceptional and ranges from 4 to 6 feet tall. The 'Pacific Coast Strains' are even taller and will produce blooming stems almost 6 feet in height. For less ambitious sites, *Delphinium* 'Magic Fountains' is a little more demure at 3 feet.

Cultural Information: Delphiniums are heavy feeders and demand a deep, rich, well-drained soil to which copious amounts of organic matter have been added. If you do not have the wherewithal to double dig your entire garden site, double dig for your delphiniums. Delphiniums appreciate an application of ground agricultural lime, bone meal or wood ash to sweeten the soil as they don't care for acid soils.

Plants are typically started from seed. Seed where they are to grow in spring, or seed them in fall, transplanting in spring. Many nurseries and greenhouses offer them as well.

Delphinium *will provide a grand display of flowers for the garden and vase. A few spikes harvested and conditioned will combine with peonies for a breathtaking arrangement.*

Dianthus 'Spring Beauty' will provide years of enjoyment in the garden. They do best in a well-drained, slightly alkaline soil.

Dianthus 'Helen' will seem much more fragrant indoors where its beauty can be appreciated more closely.

Echinacea purpurea appears in the cutting garden, herb garden and perennial borders at Mohonk Mountain House.

Fertilize delphiniums heavily throughout the growing season, when new shoots emerge, flower buds form, after flowers are harvested, and as a second flush of growth emerges in late summer. Keep the roots moist, but never allow soggy soils to persist, as this encourages root rot. Organic mulches help discourage weeds and maintain even moisture levels in the soil, but may increase the incidence of slugs, which can be devastating. Delphiniums need a sunny place in the garden and prefer cool summer nights and moderate winters. Where ideal conditions exist, delphinium clumps will continue to grow and produce more and more flowers each year. For many of us, however, we must start each year with new seedlings and do all that we can to make them happy.

The taller strains of *Delphinium* require staking to protect the heavy flower stems from breaking away at the base in heavy winds and rains. Some gardeners stake each stem, fastening it to the stake at 1-foot intervals. For cutting purposes, however, it may be desirable to create a "corral" of stakes around each plant.

Harvest and Use: Harvest delphinium spikes by cutting the stem down to the basal foliage. At the time of harvest, fertilize with well-rotted manure or 5-10-5 slow-release fertilizer to encourage a second flush of growth that will bloom in August and September. Flower stems should be placed in hot water for conditioning overnight. Don't use shortcuts when conditioning delphiniums. The height of the spikes taxes the stems' ability to provide enough water to support them to the top. Delphiniums can be designed in floral foam for a special occasion, but for the best results use a vase with a deep reservoir that will hold a large amount of water, and keep the container full at all times; delphiniums are as demanding in the vase as in the garden. Combine the stately spikes of delphiniums with peonies. Together they are unbeatable and complement each other in every way.

Dianthus (di-ANTH-us) garden pinks, ○ C

Zones: 3 to 8

Characteristics: Garden pinks are unparalleled for scent in the garden. The evergreen tufts of gray-green foliage make them ideal edging plants for the integrated border and rockery. Perennial pinks do best in full sun and will not grow in less-than-perfect drainage. They do not require overly rich soils, thriving in sandy soils or spilling over rock walls. *D. plumarius*, the cottage pink, is a vigorous grower to 1½ feet. There are several named varieties of the cottage pink, all suitable for cutting and including in small bouquets. The single, semidouble and double forms are available in colors ranging from white to pale pink, salmon, rose and crimson.

D. deltoides, the maiden pink, grows to 1½ feet with bright green basal foliage that forms loose mats. Colors of *D. deltoides* varieties range from white through pinks and purples. Many are accented with contrasting rings of color on the single row of petals. The fragrance is distinctly clovelike and a delightful addition to any bouquet.

Cultural Information: Pinks should be grown only in full sun and perfectly drained soil. Imperfect drainage will cause crown rot and death. Pinks can be grown from seed or cuttings, and starter plants are often available at nurseries. Established clumps should be divided in spring every 3 or 4 years; discard the older centers. Soil should be slightly sweet, and pinks respond well to ground agricultural limestone. A mulch of marble chips placed around the base of each plant will improve air circulation and drainage around the plant crowns.

Harvest and Use: Condition *Dianthus* blossoms in cool water after removing lower leaves. Flowers last equally well in water and floral foam, for as long as 2 weeks. Combine pinks with bachelor's buttons in a small crystal vase for an endearingly old-fashioned arrangement. Add pinks to bouquets of lily of the valley and violets, and the heady arrangement will perfume an entire room.

Echinacea purpurea (ek-in-AY-see-a pur-PEWR-ee-a) purple coneflower, ○ ◑ ◆ ☀ H

Zones: 3–9

Characteristics: Purple coneflower turns up everywhere in the gardens at Mohonk. In the perennial border, its rosy purple, daisylike flowers bloom from June until frost. In herb gardens, *Echinacea* is an example of the medicinal herbs used in tinctures to strengthen the immune system. In cutting gardens, *Echinacea* is a prolific source of cut flowers for an extended season and into the fall, when the cone-shaped centers can be collected for use in dried bouquets. The single row of flower petals tip back gently, giving this plant a look distinctive from that of other daisies. The variety 'Bright Star' will grow to 3 feet and has rosy plum petals surrounding a lovely orange cone. 'White Swan' has pure white rays, a delightful honey scent and grows to 18 inches in the garden.

Cultural Information: Easy to grow, *Echinacea* doesn't require rich soil and will, in fact, thrive in any full sun location in well-drained average soil. Planted in spring, purple coneflower will bloom the first year; or, buy seedlings from the greenhouse or garden center. Allowing some flowers to set seed each year will increase the colony and provide for an endless supply of cuts all season long.

Harvest and Use: Cut flowers close to the basal foliage; in this way, you can get stem lengths of 18 or more inches. Condition in hot water before designing. Try purple coneflower with *Liatris* for a rough-textured, boldly colored arrangement.

Eulalia grass; see ***Misanthus***

False spirea; see ***Astilbe***

Funkia; see ***Hosta***

Gaillardia × ***grandiflora*** (gay-LARD-ee-a ex gran-di-FLO-ra) **gaillardia, blanketflower,** ○ ◗ ✳ **S, H**
Zones: 3 to 9
Characteristics: For summer bouquets and summer gardens, nothing is more rewarding than *Gaillardia*. The single flower heads are composed of brightly colored, single petals surrounding a fuzzy, rounded dark center. The petals come in a range of sunset colors and are frequently banded in multihued combinations of yellow, gold, burgundy and red. There are double and semidouble forms available.

Cultural Information: Gaillardia, easily grown from seed, is undemanding of soils and does best in rather poor soils that are perfectly drained. Sow the seed in spring after all danger of frost, or up to 2 months before frost in fall. *Gaillardia* detest cold, wet, heavy soils and thrive in hot, sunny locations. Although they will tolerate drought, they prefer an adequate supply of moisture. Where conditions are less than ideal, treat them like annuals and start with new seeds each year. For those of us with ideal sites, periodic division will be necessary to keep the individual plants vigorous and maintain flower production.

Harvest and Use: Harvest toward the end of your picking sessions, as the petals don't have much substance and will not recover if crushed or badly wilted. Condition in hot water, suspending the stems as described in the florist's trick on page 32. In the cool autumn months, it is wise to harvest during the warmer part of the day when stems are pulling water up from the roots. Harvest regularly to keep plants producing from July through frost. Save the centers from spent blossoms for use in dried bouquets or other crafts.

Garden pinks; see ***Dianthus***

Garden phlox; see ***Phlox***

Gayfeather; see ***Liatris***

Goldenrod; see ***Solidago***

Gooseneck loosestrife; see ***Lysimachia***

Gypsophila paniculata (jip-SOFF-ill-a pan-i-KEW-la-ta) **hardy baby's breath,** ○ **S, H**
Zones: 3 to 10
Characteristics: Gypsophila has as its root *gypsos*, Greek for "chalk." And like the word rooted in chalk, so the plant likes to be rooted—in "chalk." Baby's breath is a perennial that requires very well drained

Gaillardia grandiflora *is as useful when it's past its prime as when it's perfect. The globular seed heads can be used effectively in many arrangements.*

Gypsophila *can provide an abundance of tiny double flowers for fresh or dry use. Be sure the soil is very well drained and enriched with lime.*

soils enriched with copious amounts of ground limestone. Baby's breath, or "gyp," can reach 4 feet in height and a similar spread. It is valued for the profusion of tiny white blossoms found on wiry stems. *Cultural Information:* Grow named varieties from root divisions purchased from mail-order catalogs or purchase container-grown plants from your favorite nursery or garden center. For the border, plant them 4 feet apart toward the back, in full sun. Gyp is frequently grown near old-fashioned bleeding heart and Oriental poppies to cover the void left by the latter after their brief display of spring foliage. *Gypsophila* needs staking, and most gardeners agree the best method of supporting the profusion of tangled stems is to corset the plants in a bamboo cage held together with strong twine. The great mass of flowers will spill over the twine and do much to cover the mechanics.

Harvest and Use: Harvest masses of blossoms in full bloom for drying in a warm, dark, dry place. For fresh flowers, cut in the evening and place in buckets with generous amounts of hot water to which 2 or 3 drops of liquid detergent and 2 or 3 drops of liquid chlorine bleach have been added. The liquid detergent will assist in the absorption of water and the bleach will not only keep the water fresh and bacteria free but seems actually to whiten the flowers!

Baby's breath works well with everything. Its only drawback is that the commercial florists have used it *ad nauseum* and so we sometimes consider its use as trite. For a change of pace, try generous amounts of gyp with a few blooms of garden pinks, bachelor's buttons, *Coreopsis, Gomphrena* or other quarter-size blooms. The effect is delightfully feminine and will be pleasing at a wedding reception, bridal shower or as a gift to a new mother. One plant of baby's breath, if harvested completely, may yield as much as three full displays of blooms over the course of the growing season.

Hardy baby's breath; see *Gypsophila paniculata*

Hardy garden chrysanthemum; see *Chrysanthemum*

Hardy garden phlox; see *Phlox*

Heuchera × *brizoides*
(hew-KER-a ex bri-ZOY-deez) **coralbells, ◑ ○ C**
Zones: 4 to 8
Characteristics: I think we all have sentimental favorites.

Heuchera will always remind me of my first gardening job at the house down the street, where in partial shade the coralbells grew lushly. I learned at 10 years of age that flowers don't have to be huge neon signs boldly crying out their glories to be of value. Coralbells are North American natives grown for their handsome, evergreen foliage and delicate racemes of tiny coral, pink, red or white blossoms. The leaves are rounded or kidney shaped, frequently mottled, veined or banded in white or maroon. *H. micratha diversifolia* 'Palace Purple' is a new cultivar to the garden scene and has already won acclaim for its deep purple-bronze foliage, which is deeply lobed, shiny above and bright red below. The flowers and foliage are excellent cuts, suitable together, of course, or in mixed flower bouquets.

Cultural Information: Most *Heuchera* can be grown successfully from seed. Named varieties may be purchased from nurseries and mail-order catalogs. The Bressingham hybrids will grow to 18 inches and provide plenty of flowers for cutting in the full color range. 'Palace Purple' is reliable from seed; plant the seed in partial shade in well-drained garden soil ammended with lots of organic matter. Do not cover the seed because it needs to be exposed to light to germinate. Coralbells will bloom the second year, starting in June, with sporadic repeat bloom throughout the summer. Bareroot plants are available, as are container-grown plants of many varieties each spring. Divide

Heuchera 'Palace Purple' has wonderful burgundy foliage that can be harvested for use with many flowers. Consider using it with coreopsis for a bold scheme.

coralbells every 4 to 5 years to avoid overcrowding. Be careful not to bury the crown with applications of organic matter or dense protective winter mulches, as crown rot will follow. A light protective mulching of pine straw or evergreen boughs should be applied after the ground has frozen to avoid frost heaving and protect evergreen foliage. When removing the mulch in spring, take the time to clean away dead leaves of *Heuchera* or other organic debris.

Harvest and Use: Harvest by cutting back to the base any flower stems as they start to open; condition in cool water. Coralbells combine nicely with shasta daisies, and seem a natural pairing with columbines. Try mixing the leaves of 'Palace Purple' with the flowers of coreopsis for a strong statement of color.

Hosta (HOS-ta) plantain lily, funkia, hosta, ● ◐ W

Zones: 3 to 9

Characteristics: Hosta is a large genus with many exciting variations suitable for growing in the deepest shade. Unfortunately, few people remember the lowly hosta when it comes time to create flower arrangements. Try *H. plantaginea* 'Royal Standard' for its smooth green leaves and deliciously fragrant blossoms; the white flowers are held 18 inches above basal foliage mounding to 16 inches. *Hosta* 'So Sweet' is a variegated form with glossy green leaves with white margins; the white flower spikes are 24 inches tall, with individ-

ual florets that are sweetly fragrant. The variety of hostas never fails to amaze. Leaves will be small or large, narrow or broad, smooth, puckered or quilted. Leaf colors range from chartreuse to deep green, golden to blue, and many are variegated in gold, cream or startling white. Flowers borne on leafless stems may be white or, more commonly, mauve or violet. Many are fragrant.

Cultural Information: They are extremely easy to grow as long as they receive shade from the hottest sun and adequate moisture. Hostas rarely need division, and over time will form competitive root systems that discourage weeds, making them admirable groundcovers. Purchase container-grown plants from the nursery in spring, or bareroot plants, which may be ordered through the mail.

Harvest and Use: Flowers should be harvested for arranging as the first flower opens; the other buds on the stems will continue to open. Conditioning in warm water before use will encourage their ability to last. Leaves should also be conditioned before use. Place the leaf stems in warm water overnight, or submerge the entire leaves in a pan of warm water for 30 minutes before standing up in water. This also washes off dust and pollen that frequently dull the shiny, broad leaves.

The tubular- to trumpet-shaped flowers look well with the rounded forms of dahlias. Try variegated hosta foliage with an all-white flower arrangement—very cool, sophisticated and summery.

Hosta *(here, 'Honey Bells')* can provide not only foliage but fragrance and beauty from their flowers.

Hosta fortunei *'Aureo-marginata'* has green leaves boldly accented with gold. Consider playing upon this theme and building an arrangement of golds and greens with accents of deep blue.

Lance coreopsis; see *Coreopsis*

Lavandula officinalis (lav-AN-dew-la of-fiss-IN-al-is) lavender, ○ ◆ W

Zones: 5 to 9

Characteristics: Lavender is considered an herb, and rightly so; for centuries, lavender has been grown to scent linens, create perfumes and repel insects, and it has been eaten fresh in salads and dried in culinary herb mixtures. The delicate lavender blue spikes are ideal for the home cutting garden. Lavender adds not only beauty but distinctive fragrance to bouquets.

Lavender brings to mind clean, crisp images and was a favorite of our grandmothers. The flowers and silvery foliage of Lavandula officinalis both offer strong scent.

Liatris spicata *is a native American prairie flower. Give it a location in full sun and you will raise flowers excellent for cutting.*

Strong stems and grey-green foliage are what makes Lychnis coronaria *an excellent choice for garden and vase.*

Lavender will bloom periodically from June until frost. The variety 'Munstead', one of the most prolific bloomers, is a slightly darker blue than the common English lavender. 'Jean Davis' is considered a pink lavender (why grow pink lavender?), but it is a dull, pale, pinkish gray; I can't recommend including it in your garden unless you are collecting lavenders. Both the flowers and foliage are fragrant and suitable for use in fresh and dried bouquets.

Cultural Information: Lavender is actually a small, evergreen shrub and grows to 18 inches tall. It can be grown from seed, but usually it is easier to purchase plants. Prepare the soil in a well-drained, sunny location by adding lime, bone meal or wood ash to increase the alkalinity. Space the plants 10 to 12 inches apart for the best display and to provide plenty of room for plant growth. In the North, plants may need some light protective winter mulch to prevent die back, caused by severe temperatures or strong winter winds. If damage has occurred, cut back affected parts in spring to newly emerging buds. Lavender will bloom on new growth. Periodically side dress established plants with lime or bone meal to maintain a neutral soil pH.

Harvest and Use: Strip off only the foliage that would be submerged in water. (Save the strippings for inclusion in potpourri, or simply set them out in a basket to enjoy the fragrance.) Use warm to hot water to condition the flower stems, anywhere from 6 to 10 inches in length. Consider mixing lavender with other delicately fragrant flowers such as roses, garden pinks or lily of the valley in a small vase to brighten the room of a bed-ridden friend; the fragrance will do as much to lift the spirits and promote healing as the beauty will.

Lavender; see ***Lavandula***

Liatris spicata (lee-AT-riss spik-AH-ta) **gayfeather,** ○ ❋ **W**

Zones: 3 to 9

Characteristics: Liatris is a native American from the prairie states. It is bold and rather coarse—in other words, perfect for making a bright statement in your flower design. From heavy, mostly basal foliage emerge dense spikes of fuzzy, magenta-purple flowers. The spikes of some varieties will grow to 6 feet. They are distinctive in that they open from the top down, the opposite of how snapdragons and gladioluses open.

Cultural Information: Plant *Liatris* corms or young, nursery-grown plants in a sunny location. Good drainage is important; although they will thrive in copious amounts of moisture during the height of the growing season, they will disappear from the garden if soils are soggy during the winter months. An annual side dressing of 5-10-5 slow-release fertilizer will keep them happy and healthy.

'Kolbold' has 2-foot spikes of slightly deeper purple than the species. 'White Spires' (*L. scariosa*) is a 3-foot white form that can be useful in the garden. The Kansas gayfeather is the tallest of the genus (*L. pycnostacha*), growing to 6 feet with a somewhat more open flowering spike. In wetter soils or windy locations it may be necessary to provide support for the tallest gayfeathers, but most will be fine without staking.

When harvesting, leave as much foliage as possible on the plants to feed the roots. *Liatris* does not need regular dividing, but note that diminished flower size or production may indicate overcrowding. Divide the cormous roots with a sharp knife and discard the oldest, woody portion of each plant.

Harvest and Use: After conditioning in warm water, *Liatris* can be combined with all manner of flowers from the garden. Purple *Liatris* and bright yellow 'Connecticut King' lilies is a bold-as-brass combination suitable for a large centerpiece. *Liatris* with cosmoses and purple coneflowers is a more subtle approach, though equally enjoyable.

Lily of the valley; see ***Convallaria***

Loosestrife, gooseneck; see ***Lysimachia***

Lychnis coronaria (lik-NISS ko-ro-NAY-ree-a) **mullein pink, rose campion,** ○ ❋ ◗ **H**

Zones: 4 to 8

Characteristics: This delightfully old-fashioned perennial favorite is easy to grow and will provide bold, hot pink to magenta blossoms throughout summer into fall. The mostly basal, pubescent gray foliage shows off these bright flowers.

Cultural Information: A seed packet planted in full sun in spring will provide a lifetime supply of plants and flowers. The plants themselves are short lived but reseed readily, creating colonies of plants. Unwanted seedlings can be rogued out, transplanted elsewhere or given away. *Lychnis c.* 'Alba' is a white-flowered form; 'Angel Blush' is a seed mix with a color range from white to cerise, most of the plants white with pinkish centers.

Harvest and Use: Hot water should be used to condition flower stems, which will last up to 1 week. The stems are multibudded and 18 to 24 inches tall. Combine the hot pink forms with white or silver foliage. Try *Lychnis* massed with *Artemisia ludoviciana* 'Silver King'.

Lysimachia clethroides

(li-si-MAK-ee-a kleth-ROY-deez) **gooseneck loosestrife,** ○ ◑ **W**

Zones: 4 to 9

Characteristics: Plant this one and step back! Gooseneck is more than gregarious, more than aggressive—it is invasive. The 3-foot-high plants are topped with white spikes of little flowers. Each spike bends in the middle and the tip faces up, giving the overall impression of a goose neck.

Cultural Information: Whether planted in full sun or partial shade, the vigorous rhizomatic root system of gooseneck will spread like wildfire. Choose a location for this where its groundcoverlike habit will not cause trouble. Gooseneck will do best in sites with plenty of

moisture. Prepare any good garden soil with generous amounts of organic matter.

Harvest and Use: Don't be afraid to harvest gooseneck stems right back to the ground; this plant has enough energy to support the loss of foliage. Strip the foliage by grasping loosely and pulling it down toward the base of the stem. Condition cut and cleaned gooseneck in warm water overnight. The joy is in its wonderful line, and the slightly arching flower spikes provide charm and interest to any arrangement. Combine it with blossoms from any mixture of summer-flowering annuals: snapdragons, cosmos, zinnias and lisianthus (*Eustoma*) will all benefit from the association.

Michaelmas daisy; see *Aster*

Miscanthus sinensis

(mis-KAN-thus syn-EN-sis) **eulalia grass,** ○ ◑ **W**

Zones: 4 to 9

Characteristics: Miscanthus is an excellent ornamental grass for gardeners who don't want an invasive grass filling their flower borders. It has some endearing qualities for the floral designer as well—gently recurved tips create little pig tails. The grass plumes have a shimmering pink quality when fresh, and when mature and dry, *Miscanthus* has wonderfully fluffy white plumes suitable for use in bouquets fresh or dried.

M. sinensis 'Gracillimus' has green and yellow stripes (variegation) that follow the vertical parallel veins of the grass blades. *M. sinensis* 'Zebrinus',

Lysimachia clethroides is typified by a gracefully arched spire of pure white flowers. Gooseneck may be invasive in the garden and should be planted where it can colonize.

the zebra grass, is variegated with gold banding across the leaf blade.

Cultural Information: Miscanthus is easy to grow and will adapt well to almost any garden situation. For best results plant in full sun in rich, moist soils. But, consider *Miscanthus* for use in trouble spots, wet locations, dry locations and full sun, too. It never needs dividing and will produce more blooms each year.

Harvest and Use: The flower plumes can be harvested when fresh or dry and need not be conditioned. The leaf blades of *Miscanthus* should be condi-

Many ornamental grasses are valuable in the border and should not be overlooked for inclusion in the cutting garden. Miscanthus sinensis (background) has silvery white panicles in autumn on 4-foot plants. Pennisetum alopecuroides (foreground) will also provide plenty of flower heads for fresh and dry use.

tioned in warm water before use. Try the dried plumes with freshly cut hardy mums or asters. The unripened flower heads are shown off to perfection against the deep colors of dark-hued *Salvia*, the bronzed foliage of autumn peonies, and mahogany sunflowers.

Monarda didyma (mo-NAR-da di-DEE-ma) **bee balm, bergamot, Oswego tea,** ○ ◗ H

Zones: 4 to 9

Characteristics: This fine garden perennial was used by Native Americans for making tea, hence one of the common names, Oswego tea. Bee balm is a wildflower of meadows and roadsides, where its unusual flowers are usually pale lilac.

Bee balm is a member of the mint family and its active rootstocks will form dense clumps and may become invasive. This plant will do well in full sun or light shade, in moist or dry soils. The flowers are borne in terminal clusters and are frequently surrounded by brightly colored rings of bracts. The color range extends from white through pink and red to violet. To enjoy this summer-blooming perennial fully, plant it where you can watch the hummingbirds that will come to feed on the sweet nectar.

Cultural Information: Bee balm is nearly always grown from root division, a means of reproduction that produces specimens identical to the mother plant. Mildew is a problem with *Monarda*, and care should be taken to plant in an area with good air circulation. For greatest success, plant in rich garden

Monarda didyma is a member of the mint family, and its flower clusters will attract hummingbirds and bees. Divide Monarda every year to keep plants young and vigorous.

Nothing compares with Paeonia *for beauty of fragrance and form. Plant extras for bountiful June bloom and superb cut foliage throughout the growing season.*

soil with abundant moisture and divide every 2 to 3 years, eliminating the oldest, woody portions of the root stocks. This is best done in spring, and presents an opportunity to enrich the soil with well-rotted manure or compost.

Harvest and Use: Harvest bee balm from your cutting garden regularly to stretch the blooming period to 2 months or longer. Flowers should be stripped of their foliage and conditioned in hot water. Clean, disease-free (unsprayed) leaves can be steeped in boiling water to make an aromatic and refreshing beverage. Try *Monarda* 'Blue Stocking' in arrangements with white garden phlox and yellow coreopsis. The reds and pinks ('Cambridge Scarlet' or 'Croftway Pink') work well in combination with blue larkspurs and lisianthus.

Monkshood; see *Aconitum*

Mugwort; see *Artemisia*

Mullein pink; see *Lychnis*

Oswego tea; see *Monarda*

Paeonia lactifolia (pie-ON-ee-a lac-ti-FOL-ee-a) **peony,** ○ ◗ ✳ W

Zones: 3–8

Characteristics: This herbaceous plant is truly the queen of the garden. It is long lived, relatively pest free, and creates some of the most stunning, exquisitely fragrant flower arrangements. Peonies may be single, fully double or anenome flowered, and the flowers pure white, deep red, or any shade of pink from coral to raspberry.

Cultural Information: Peonies are exacting in their site requirements, but once established they are long lived, undemanding perennials. Choose a sunny location where the soil is deep, well drained and free from tree roots. Peonies dislike disturbance and competition. Do not crowd them with plants that will compete for air, light and nutrients, nor should you place them near annuals where the soil will be dug every year.

Peonies are best divided in late summer, and the largest selection is available at that time of year. (Too often we think to plant flowers when we see them in bloom in other peoples' gardens.) Plants that are container grown will be available in spring, but typically the variety selection is poorer than catalog selections. Prepare the soil well, adding steamed bone meal to hasten early root formation. Plant the tuberous roots about 1½ inches deep and water in well. Provide a mulch once the ground has frozen the first winter to prevent frost heaving. Young peonies benefit from an application of balanced slow-release fertilizer in the spring.

Harvest and Use: Peony blossoms can be harvested from the time the buds begin to show color, when they are about the size of golf balls. They will open in the vase, so cutting them young will extend your enjoyment. Cut the stems only as long as you need them to minimize unnecessary foliage loss, though taking the occasional stem back to the ground on a mature peony will not damage the plant. Don't overlook the single peony; not only is it a lovely cut, with its bright yellow stamens, but the singles frequently have fewer disease problems in the garden. The doubles may collect water in the petals during spring rains, causing the plants to break over and botrytis (gray mold) to proliferate.

Condition cut stems in warm water overnight. Don't discard leaves from the peony; they are long-lasting in arrangements. Peony foliage can be cut from mature peonies any time during the season for use in bouquets; it is attractive and holds up nicely. I especially like peony foliage in the autumn when it becomes bronzed. Try bronze peony foliage with orange and yellow American marigolds.

Peonies are ideal design subjects in any number of combinations. Three peonies of any color with an armload of lilacs is all you need to create fragrant magic. Try white, single peonies with delphiniums of deep blue, or mass peonies and mountain laurel cuttings for an elegant centerpiece.

Painted daisy; see ***Chrysanthemum***

Peony; see ***Paeonia***

Phlox paniculata (FLOX pan-i-KEW-la-ta) hardy garden phlox, ○ ◖ H

Zones: 3 to 9

Characteristics: Phlox reminds me of sunny August days spent vacationing in Maine; masses of pink, white and magenta blooms spilling through white picket fences by seaside cottages is still a vivid image for me. Phlox is an easy-to-grow perennial and can be the mainstay of the late-summer flower border.

Cultural Information: Plants are propagated by root cuttings in spring and should be planted out in the garden in full sun to light shade. Where still, humid days are common, watch out for mildew, which can disfigure foliage and weaken

Phlox (here, Phlox paniculata *'Starfire') is a wonderful flower for the late-summer border and vase. Divide the plants regularly and choose varieties that resist mildew.*

plants. Look for resistant varieties at your favorite nursery. Plant cuttings or young plants into freshly prepared soil to which organic matter has been added. Plant 15 to 18 inches apart with the eyes (buds) just below the soil surface. A light organic mulch will help conserve moisture and reduce weeds.

As plants mature, they weaken and so benefit from dividing. Choose only the most vigorous of the new shoots each spring and space them out in newly enriched soil. It may be necessary to control mildew during some seasons; if mildew is caught early, a fungicidal application will help curb the disease. In the garden, be very conscientious with fall cleanup. Remove any diseased foliage from the base of plants and destroy or discard it—do not compost it. Harvesting flowers for arrangements and bouquets prolongs bloom, but it is a good idea to deadhead phlox to prevent reseeding and varieties that may revert to the common, muddy magenta.

Harvest and Use: After stripping off the lower foliage from cut phlox, condition it in a deep container of hot water. Bouquets of phlox with *Aconitum*, hot pink phlox with *Hydrangea paniculata* or just armloads of phloxes all by themselves will prove to be beautiful additions to any decor.

Pinks, garden; see ***Dianthus***

Plantain lily; see ***Hosta***

Purple coneflower; see ***Echinacea***

Rose campion; see ***Lychnis***

Shasta daisy; see ***Chrysanthemum***

Solidago (so-lid-AH-go) **goldenrod,** ○ ◐ ◆ H
Zones: 2 to 9
Characteristics: The goldenrods are often maligned—and unfairly—as the source of hayfever and have been shunned for years. The tall, stately spires of this bright golden native American should be included in every summer border where their sunny color and hardy disposition will cheer even the dourest heart. Goldenrod is a hardy perennial that forms vigorous clumps of mostly basal foliage and gently curved flower spikes up to 6 feet.
Cultural Information: Choose a sunny location for this gregarious member of the composite (daisy) family. It is easily propagated from root division. Be sure to deadhead to avoid unwanted seedlings. Much breed-

A weed is a plant out of place, but Solidago *'Crown of Rays' deserves a place in every garden.*

ing work has been done in Europe where *Solidago* is grown for use in borders and is frequently seen in the flower shops. 'Cloth of Gold' has deep yellow flower heads on 2-foot stems. *S.* × 'Peter Pan' is a late-blooming variety and slightly taller, at 2½ to 3 feet.
Harvest and Use: Don't neglect the roadsides where goldenrod abounds. Cut it as it begins to open and it will dry beautifully and maintain its glorious golden color. Harvest whole stems and strip off the foliage. The stems will condition and become turgid if placed in hot water overnight. After conditioning, use them in masses all by themselves or with cattails or dried grasses. For a bolder look, arrange goldenrod with the smaller-flowered sunflowers in old crocks.

Speedwell; see ***Veronica***

Spirea, false; see ***Astilbe***

Tanacetum vulgare (tan-ah-SEE-tum vul-GAR-ee) **tansy,** ○ ◐ H
Zones: 4 to 10
Characteristics: Tansy is a versatile composite with lovely, fernlike foliage and broad heads of buttonlike, bright yellow flowers.
Cultural Information: Grow tansy in full sun in average garden soil. At Mohonk, we grow tansy in our herb garden because it acts as a natural insect repellant. Try *T. vulgare* 'Crispum' for its tight, crisp foliage, as well as the species. Both of these grow to 3 feet in height and produce abundant flowers. Sow seed in autumn, or plant root divisions or nursery-grown specimens in spring. Do not try to create a rich soil for tansy as it will become invasive, overly lush, and require staking.
Harvest and Use: Harvest tansy with long stems. As you strip off the foliage, save some for use in arrangements and add

Tanacetum vulgare is a delightful specimen for the herb garden, where it is grown for its insect repellant properties. The yellow buttons borne atop 2¹/2-foot stems are ideal for use in fresh and everlasting arrangements.

the rest to a natural moth-repellant potpourri with lavender, thyme and rosemary. Tansy should be placed in containers of hot water for conditioning. Combine it with other late-summer perennials or annuals such as *Aconitum*, asters and *Celosia*. Be sure to harvest some to dry, hung upside down in a dark, dry, warm location.

Tansy; see ***Tanacetum***

Tickseed; see ***Coreopsis***

Veronica spicata (vu-RON-i-cah spi-CAH-ta) **speedwell**, ○ ◐ ☀ ◕ **W**

Zone: 3–10

Characteristics: Veronica is an easy, free-blooming perennial for the foreground of the sunny, integrated border or cutting garden. The delicate spikes of blue, violet, rose, pink or white are ideal subjects for smaller arrangements and small-scale gardens. *Veronica* grows to 15 to 24 inches tall and produces spikes as much as 1 foot long. *Cultural Information:* Plant *Veronica* in rich, well-drained soil 1 to 2 feet apart. The plants are exceptionally heat and drought tolerant. Most varieties need no staking. By regularly harvesting flowers, you can extend the season of bloom for several weeks.

Harvest and Use: Try 'Minuet', which has rich pink blooms in July, or 'Sunny Border Blue', with intense blue flower spikes. Condition the flower stems in warm water. Try *Veronica* with *Dianthus* or *Nigella*. The rosy pink forms can be prettily used with *Lychnis* 'Angel Blush'. Try 'Sunnyborder Blue' with pale yellow *Calendula* and chive blossoms.

Wormwood; see ***Artemisia***

Yarrow; see ***Achillea***

Veronica spicata *(here, 'Minuet') comes in a variety of colors, from blue to pink to white.*

BULBS, CORMS, TUBERS AND RHIZOMES

Acidanthera bicolor (ah-sid-ANTH-e-ra by-COL-or) **peacock orchid, dark-eye gladixia**, ○ ☀ **W**

Zone: 10

Characteristics: Bright white butterflies blotched with chocolate brown and black, the flowers of *Acidanthera* are borne above the swordlike foliage from July until frost in the sunny garden.

Cultural Information: Acidanthera is related to the gladiola and requires similar culture, but it offers an unusually exotic cut flower for late-summer bouquets. The fragrant flowers will continue to be formed on the loosely branching stems throughout autumn. *Acidanthera* is easy to grow in average soil in full sun. It is native to Ethiopia, and enjoys summer heat. In warmer climates it will overwinter without being dug and stored. In the Northeast it is necessary to dig, clean and store the corms over winter.

After the foliage has been killed back by frost, carefully dig up the corms. Cut back the stem to within 2 inches of the corm and remove any fibrous roots. Allow the coarse, papery cover to remain. Store in peat moss or sawdust in a cool, slightly damp location until spring. Plant outdoors where they are to grow after danger of frost is past. As you lift the mature corms, watch for cormels (baby corms); these may be grown on in a nursery row for two seasons until they reach blooming size.

Harvest and Use: Harvest by removing individual flowers, entire stems or entire plants, depending on the length of stem desired. Pulling the plant from the ground and cutting the corm off at the base of the stem will give you the greatest stem length for designing, but will sacrifice the corm, which must be discarded. Cut stems should be placed in warm water in a container deep enough to support the flower spikes. After conditioning, combine with dahlias for a lovely display. I like the exotic look of individual buds, leaves and full blossoms of *Acidanthera* arranged in hollowed-out eggplants. Clustered together on a pewter platter or in a handsome flat basket, the eggplants and peacock orchids complement each other in form and color, making an elegant centerpiece for a summer Sunday brunch.

Acidanthera bicolor murielae *is best treated like its relative, the gladiolus. The fragrant white flowers with chocolate-purple throats are topped by gently nodding buds waiting to open.*

Allium caeruleum is an important color accent in this arrangement of green, chartreuse and creamy white. Alliums are easy to grow in most garden soils.

Crocosmia is easily grown and will produce an abundance of flowers suitable for cutting.

Allium (AL-ee-um) **flowering onion, giant allium, chives,** ○ ✳ **C**

Zones: 2 to 8

Characteristics: The genus *Allium* is made up of the onion family. They are not only valuable culinary herbs and vegetables but are delightful additions to the perennial border, cutting garden and arrangements. Don't worry about onion breath from your centerpieces ruining a dinner party, though; alliums lose their onion scent once the cut stems are conditioned. The variety of sizes in the garden is worth noting: *A. schoenoprasum* (chives) are about 12 inches tall with 2-inch blossoms, whereas *A. giganteum* (the giant allium) will top out at 4 to 5 feet tall with flower heads 6 or more inches across. *A. giganteum* is only marginally hardy in northern gardens, so it is critical that it be planted in a perfectly drained soil; a winter mulch of evergreen boughs, pine straw or straw will help protect it from severe cold. *A. sphaerocephalum* (drumstick allium) has 2-inch heads of tightly clustered blossoms that are deep violet when open and bright green in the bud. This is an excellent, long-lasting cut with 2-foot stems, and one of the least expensive of the alliums. Plant plenty of these in the garden for fresh and dry use. *A. caeruleum* (blue garlic) is one of the finest of the alliums, easy to grow and hardy. Blue garlic will produce 1-inch balls of bright cornflower blue on 2-foot stems in June.

Cultural Information: Alliums need a sunny garden site with well-drained soil. They will accept poor garden soils and live for season after season, but poor drainage will cause them to fail. The foliage of alliums is basal. Some, like the giant allium, are flat and hug the ground; chives are tubular and upright. Most of the foliage has a lovely blue-green cast and is a delightful garden accent. Plant enough alliums for fresh and dried use. Chives are usually sold as plants in spring; all other alliums should be purchased in autumn and planted in September or early October. Plant bulbs in well-prepared soil enriched with organic matter and bone meal, which will encourage early root formation. Some alliums will produce growth in autumn, but this won't hurt flower formation or display.

Harvest and Use: Harvest blossoms when they are about halfway open, as they will continue to mature in the vase. Condition alliums in cool water to help reduce any oniony fragrance. Giant alliums are handsome with white delphiniums or yellow lilies. The chives are ideal in bouquets of herbs and other edible flowers such as rose buds, nasturtiums and *Calendula*. There is no limit to the floral combinations for this delightfully easy perennial bulb.

Chive; see *Allium*

Crocosmia (kro-KOS-mee-a) **crocosmia, montbretia,** ○ ◑ ✳ **W**

Zones: 7 to 10

Characteristics: Crocosmia is a tender bulb sold in spring. In northern gardens it is treated like a tender annual. In gardens south of Zone 6 it can be left in the ground where it will colonize and behave as a perennial. This African native is available in shades of yellow, orange and bright, bold red. The flowers are borne on strong stems 15 to 20 inches tall in August and September. Typically, the flower stems branch and curve slightly, the ends of the spikes bearing a couple rows of buds, very much like freesia.

Cultural Information: Plant *Crocosmia* in spring in a sunny or partially shady location when soils are warm. Plant at least 10 bulbs for a suitable display in the integrated garden, with an additional 10 for cutting. Mulch the planting during the first winter for extra insulation or, if you garden in the North, lift and store as you would gladiolas.

Harvest and Use: Harvest only as much stem length as you need for your vase arrangement. By leaving some buds on the branched, leafless stems, you can continue to produce more blooms. Condition in warm water for use with variegated grasses, zinnias and *Monarda.* Try combinations of goosenecks with crocosmias as their shapes are so similar.

Daffodil; see *Narcissus*

Dahlia (DAH-lee-a) **dahlia, ○ S,W**
Zones: 9 to 10
Characteristics: The native American dahlia is a popular, old-fashioned garden favorite. Dahlias offer a range of colors from pure white to yellow, orange, red, pink, lilac and burgundy. Many bicolors are available with contrasting striped or banded petals. Although all dahlias cut well and last in water, not all are suitable for use in bouquets. The decorative dahlias may produce blooms the size of dinner plates, but how do you use them in bouquets? For flower arrangements, choose the water-lily types, with flowers 3 to 4 inches across on plants 3½ to 4 feet tall. These upward-facing dahlias are wonderfully shaped with gently curved, clearly defined petals, on strong stems. The pompon types will produce lovely, rounded blossoms 2 to 3 inches across on plants 3 feet tall.
Cultural Information: Dahlias like plenty of moisture in deep, fertile, well-drained soil. They may need staking to stand upright in the middle or background of the sunny border or cutting garden. Dahlias may be started indoors in flats of potting soil mixed with peat moss 2 to 3 weeks before the last spring frost, then planted out when growth starts. In fall, allow the frost to kill back the plants and then dig the tubers. Cut the stems back to within 2 inches of the tubers, which should then be washed free of soil, allowed to dry and stored in peat moss or sawdust in a cool, damp area.
Harvest and Use: Cut stems of dahlias should be briefly conditioned in very hot (almost boiling water) for 5 minutes before conditioning in warm water. I like combining the water-lily dahlias in delicate pastel shades with summer annuals—bronze snapdragons with yellow or pink dahlias are delightful. The startling white dahlias are a beautiful addition to bouquets of red *Celosia* and *Hydrangea paniculata.*

Dark-eye gladixia; see *Acidanthera*

Flowering onion; see *Allium*

Gladiolus (glad-E-o-lis) **gladiola, ○ W**
Zones: 9 to 10
Characteristics: The poor *Gladiolus* has been given a bad rap. For years it has been persistently used for funeral flowers and so has become associated with bereavement. It is unfortunate that a flower that has so much to offer the flower enthusiast, with a broad color range, stately presence and long-lasting flower spikes, should be shunned. "Glads" can be pure white to deep blue, with yellows, pinks, corals and oranges filling out the spectrum. The yellows range from the palest cream to deep gold and even greenish. Plant breeders have developed some varieties with spots and blotched throats and

I find the smaller-scaled dahlia flower heads, such as the Pompon Dahlia 'Potgieter' here, easier to use in arrangements.

Even dwarf forms such as Dahlia 'Bonnie Esperance' can provide the terrace gardener a few flowers for a vase.

Gladiolus *come in every color of the rainbow, and some the rainbow has yet to see. Easy to grow and rewarding, a few "glads" make a strong color statement in an arrangement.*

Iris are long-lived perennials that form dense clumps. Cut iris blooms when they begin to unfurl and they will last well in water. (Iris germanica 'Gay Parade').

others with heavily ruffled petals more magnificent than any orchid. Plants range in height from 3 to 4 feet for standard "glads," and 2 to 3 feet for the miniature gladiola. The sword-like foliage is a bold accent to the integrated cutting garden, where "glads" should be massed for greatest affect.

Cultural Information: Gladiolus is easy to grow in any soil in full sun. Choose corms that are large and firm but not dry and rock hard to the touch. For best results, prepare the soil deeply, incorporating leaf mold or compost to increase water-holding capacity. Gladiolas should be planted in groups over a period of weeks, starting when the ground can be worked in spring and completing the last planting about the Fourth of July. Staggering the planting dates will stagger the blooming period and give you a supply of flowers from July until frost.

Just before planting soak corms in a Lysol solution (1 tablespoon Lysol to 1 gallon warm water) to control thrips and disease. Beware of thrips, minute insects that cause tan, vertical stripes along the length of gladiola leaves, mottle flowers and destroy plantings. To avoid thrips, rotate planting sites annually, and discard any suspect corms. In areas exposed to wind be prepared to support plantings with individual stakes or 4 × 4-inch support wire fixed horizontally about 1½ feet off the ground.

Harvest and Use: When harvesting gladiolas, cut the thick stems just above the foliage. Consider sacrificing the occasional corm by pulling the entire plant out of the ground and cutting the stem at the corm. (This is how commercial growers harvest gladiolus with extra-long stems.) Flowers and foliage are easily conditioned in warm water. Before use, remove the last few flower buds to encourage all the florets to open. Where flower stems are too long, cut the spike into sections and use two florets here, three there and the budded tip somewhere else. I think masses of gladiolas with their natural foliage look best. Try white and pink gladiolas with hydrangeas in autumn, or lilies with gladiolas for summer bouquets. For smaller-scale gardens, and smaller, easier-to-use flower spikes, 'Tiny Tots' will give you miniature gladiolas with 18- to 20-inch flower spikes.

Iris (EYE-ris) iris, ○ ◑ W
Zones: 3–10

Characteristics: The irises are a diverse group of plants from all over the world. There are two groups that seem particularly to shine for use in the vase. The bearded or German iris is widely hybridized and offers the enthusiast an incredible assortment of flower colors and combinations with bicolors and heavily ruffled petals abounding. I'm still drawn to the smaller-flowered, old-fashioned varieties that used to grace grandmother's garden. The Japanese iris is an outstanding cut flower and will thrive in wet places (even along the edge of a shallow pond); it ranges in color from white to purple, and may have variegation, veining or blotches in a contrasting shade, often yellow.

Cultural Information: All irises are relatively easy to grow and, once planted, will be part of the garden for many years. Bearded irises have shallow-rooted rhizomes requiring a perfectly drained location for success. Plant in full sun, and take the time to encorporate organic matter into the soil. Bearded irises are available in September and should be planted as soon as they are received. The rhizome can be left slightly exposed, but it may be helpful to use a flat rock to weight the rhizome the first winter to avoid frost heaving. Bearded irises are prone to iris borer, an insect that can be devastating. It is wise to lift and divide rhizomes every 3 to 4 years to provide them with fresh soil. Cut out any signs of borers with a sharp knife. If borers are present, transplant the irises into fresh soil in a new location in the garden.

Japanese irises are at home in wet locations in the garden; don't attempt these in dry soils as failure is ensured. The soil should be rich in organic matter and free from lime. Plant the stout rhizomes in fall and be prepared to divide every 3 to 4 years.

Harvest and Use: Irises are easy to cut and use. Choose young blooms that are just starting to open, and harvest the entire stem, taking with it three or more buds. Although not especially long lasting as a cut flower, the bearded iris will continue its display in the vase as buds open along the prepared stem. Bearded iris can remain showy in an arrangement for up to 1 week. The Japanese iris will also last for 1 week in water if harvested as the flowers start to emerge from the bud. Both are easily conditioned in warm water before being combined with other garden flowers in arrangements. I like the flowers of bearded iris alone in a vase. Be prepared to do a little house-keeping, as the faded flowers should be picked off of the stem. Try combining the purple bearded irises with peonies or Japanese irises with shasta daisies.

Jonquil; see *Narcissus*

Lilium (LIL-ee-um) **lily,** ○ ◐ **W**
Zones: 5 to 9
Characteristics: The lilies are the grand ladies of the garden, tall, stately and elegant. There are many species within this genus of hardy perennial bulbs. The Asiatic hybrids make some of the finest cut flowers. Bred for their upward-facing blooms, the Asiatic, or Hardy, hybrids range in height from 2 to 5 feet. The color range of Asiatic lilies, which bloom in June and July, seems to expand each year. Look for white, pink, yellow, red and mauve. Many of the blossoms, from 4 to 6 inches across, will be freckled with brown or purple, adding interest to their bright, clear colors. 'Enchantment' remains one of the best oranges. Try 'Connecticut Lemonglow' for an unsurpassed yellow and 'Bianca' for its ethereal white flowers.

The Oriental lilies are a little more difficult to grow, but offer fragrance, form and color not seen in other lilies. They are later to bloom in the garden, not making an appearance until August and September. Typically shorter than their Asiatic cousins, the white, pink

and cerise blossoms are wonderfully bright with their knobby petals frequently spotted. Try the pure white 'Casa Blanca' or the beautiful pink 'Stargazer'.
Cultural Information: Lilies are generally easy to grow and are long lived in the proper garden site. Choose a position in full sun or light shade and prepare the soil deeply in fall. Use plenty of organic matter and incorporate some bone meal to encourage early root development. Soil for lilies must be perfectly drained for long-term survival and colonization. Lily bulbs are delicate, unprotected bulbs. Look them over before planting them; they should be large, and their multiple layers of scales should be clean, light colored, and free from scars and rot. Plant the bulbs 5 to 6 inches deep. Lilies are best planted in fall but may not be available until early spring. Plant lily bulbs as soon as you purchase them in fall or spring for best garden performance.
Harvest and Use: Like other bulbs, lilies should be cut with a minimum of foliage. Remove no more than one-third of the lily foliage if you don't want to reduce flower displays in future years. Lily stems should be cut when the first blossom or two has opened. The remaining buds will open in the vase. Take the time after harvesting to remove the pollen-heavy anthers, as they can stain. Remove the lower leaves and place stems in warm water to condition. Lilies can be used as individual blossoms taken from the stem or as entire stems. Try combining lilies with delphiniums or larkspurs; they are com-

patable with other spike flowers, too, such as snapdragons and gladiolas.

Lily; see *Lilium*

Montbretia; see *Crocosmia*

Narcissus (nar-SIS-sus) **daffodil, narcissus, jonquil,** ○ ◐ ✳ **S,C**
Zones: 4 to 8
Characteristics: Daffodils and narcissus are the promise of spring after a long and bleak winter. Narcissus are available in many forms, from the dwarfs suitable for the rockery, to bold and brassy trumpet daffodils. Colors range from white to green, yellow, orange and pink,

Lilium 'Enchantment', one of many Asiatic hybrids available for gardeners today, is one of the finest cut flowers.

Narcissus, daffodils and jonquils all belong to the genus Narcissus. Varieties such as 'Accent' are lovely additions to the landscape and will form clumps, providing ever more flowers with each passing year.

and many offer contrasting trumpet and petal colors. The selection of varieties is seemingly endless, with large trumpets, small trumpets, single and double forms, and single and multiple blooms per head. Daffodils will bloom early, mid-season and late, with a bloom time from late March through May. They are easy to force for winter bloom indoors.

Cultural Information: Daffodils are among the hardiest of all the spring-flowering bulbs and are notoriously long-lived perennials, returning each spring for many years. Planted in a deep, rich, well-drained soil, daffodils and narcissus can be naturalized among groundcovers, hardy ferns and even perennials such as hostas. Beds of daffodils may pose a problem for the neat freak, as "daff" foliage will last well into July before it begins to die back for summer dormancy. This can look messy in the garden. An old gardener once taught me to braid daffodil foliage when it starts to look unattractive, and tie the tip of the braid to the base of the foliage for a nice, neat topknot of foliage. When the foliage can be pulled from the bulb with a light tug, remove the foliage and compost it. In naturalized settings, it isn't necessary to go through all the bother, as the foliage will be covered by the groundcover, fern fronds, leaves of hostas, daylilies or other growth where it will ripen naturally.

Plant firm, large bulbs in September and October for bloom the following spring. Triple-nosed bulbs will give you four or five flowers the first year. A handful of bone meal at the base of each planting hole will help promote early root formation. Commercial bulb fertilizers are well worth the investment; side dress bulb plantings with a handful each spring as new growth emerges. Daffodils will grow and bloom for many years without dividing; when the flower display begins to diminish, lift and divide bulbs before replanting in fall.

Harvest and Use: Narcissus can be a little messy to harvest but are almost always successfully conditioned in cool water. Daffodil stems will drool a clear, viscous liquid that can inhibit the lasting ability of other cut flowers. Always take the time to condition daffodils alone in their own container for at least 1 hour (overnight is better) before mixing them with other flowers. Care should be taken in harvesting "daffs" as their stems are hollow and the flower heads will not be supported by stems that are bent. Use a sharp knife or garden snips to cut stems. When designing with daffodils and narcissus, a thin, smooth stem from another plant can be inserted into the narcissus' hollow stem to allow for easier placement into pin holders or floral foam. Some florists use chenille stems (similar to large, fuzzy pipe cleaners and available from craft suppliers) to insert up the stems for added support and water absorption ability.

Combine daffodil and narcissus blooms with any of the spring-flowering bulbs such as tulips and *Scilla*, delicate stems of forget-me-nots and the emerging buds of trees and shrubs, or the brilliant flowers of forsythia. Don't forget to include a few daffodil leaves for a natural accent of foliage.

Peacock orchid; see *Acidanthera*

Tulipa (TOO-lip-a) **tulips,** ○ ◐ ✳ C
Zones: 4 to 8
Characteristics: Tulips are elegant perennial bulbs, much revered for their formal, upright habit in flower beds. The tulips are a diverse group of species and varieties in a range of heights and colors to please any palate. Look for flower colors ranging from white to deep red, yellow to brilliant orange, and violet to almost black! Variegation abounds in this genus with stripes, spots, picotee edges, and leaping, flamelike markings. Some of the species tulips may grow to only 3 to 6 inches in height, and others are much more stately, with the single late tulips topping the chart at 30 inches.

Several groups of tulips are worth including in the cutting garden. Single early or hybrid Darwin tulips reach to 24 inches tall in colors ranging from brilliant gold to deep red, with many orange and yellow-red bicolors. There are several pink varieties in the single early group that tend toward shell pink, pale orange and salmon. Single early tulips bloom in late March to early April. Triumph tulips are mid-season, blooming in mid- to late April. They boast a full range of colors and will top out at about 20 inches tall. Look for 'Garden Party', white petals with a vivid rose edging, and 'Apricot Beauty', with fragrant, pale apricot blossoms.

Single late tulips are the tallest of all. These tulips, in bloom in mid-May, are available in the full range of colors. Try combining one of the "black" tulips with pale pink or creamy yellow. Blooming at the same time are the fringed tulips with strong, pure-colored petals edged in delicate fringe, or lily-flowered tulips with their delicately pointed, vase-shaped blooms on stems that seem always to be bending in a light breeze. Parrot tulips are another addition to the late-spring cutting garden, their contorted blooms a wild blend of paisley colors with pale pinks, white and green or orange, yellow, red and green. Perhaps some of the finest of the cutting tulips, the peony-flowered or double late tulips are elegant additions to any bouquet in bold pinks, reds or white.

Cultural Information: Tulips are easy to grow in any well-drained soil. Look for bulbs that are large, free from bruises and cuts, and firm but not dried out. Prepare the planting bed with well-rotted manure, compost or peat moss, and enrich it with the addition of Bulb Booster or bone meal to enhance root development. Tulips should be planted slightly deeper than recommended (up to 8 inches deep); deeper planting prolongs their useful life. Annual additions of Bulb Booster will also help maintain vigor and flower production. Be sure to water bulbs in after planting to encourage good root development.

Harvest and Use: Harvest tulips when they are still in a fairly tight bud but fully colored. Tulips that have been allowed to open and close in the garden day after day will be worn out before they get into the vase. Cut the flower stem above the foliage or cut one or more leaves. Cutting leaves will reduce flowering in future years but the effect of the foliage in arrangements is worth it. Where maximum stem length is necessary, pull up the entire plant by the roots and cut the bulb off. This bulb will not grow next year and should be discarded. Use a bucket filled with cool water to condition flowers before use.

Tulips can be challenging to the floral designer. Their tendancy to continue to grow in the vase will disconcert and may upset a carefully composed arrangement. Tulip petals open during the day and close at night; this causes them to age faster than tulips that are kept closed. By keeping tulips cool, you can keep the petals from opening. Try adding ice to finished arrangements to chill the tulips and replenish the water supply. Another trick is to make a small vertical cut with a sharp knife just below the blossom. The incision should be ¼ to ½ inch long and should prevent the flower from opening.

Tulips can be combined with any number of flowers and foliages in bouquets. I like tulips all by themselves by the bowlful on a dining table. With forget-me-nots, forsythias or lilacs, tulips add an elegance unsurpassed by other flowers.

Tulips are reliably easy spring bulbs suitable for most cutting gardens. A variety of flower types are available, including 'Angelique', a double late-flowering pink.

Rembrandt tulips such as 'Burpee's Masterpiece Mixture' come in multicolored blends that work well in combination with many other flowers.

TREES AND SHRUBS

Any number of trees and shrubs can be grown for use in arrangements and to enhance the landscape. Your garden probably offers some woody selections suitable for the vase now. I prefer cuttings from small rather than large trees, as larger trees offer logistical problems when it comes time to harvest. Trees and shrubs not only offer suitable flowers but in many cases can be a source of dramatic, long-lasting foliages. I will identify a few favorites you may consider including in your garden. It is critical that you choose woody plants hardy in your USDA zone.

Evergreens are plants that maintain their foliage year 'round. Some turn bronze during the winter months. Evergreen foliage may be needled or broad-leaved, coarse or fine, solid or variegated. Evergreens offer the designer a wide range of foliage patterns, and colors from deep burgundy to yellow-green and blue-gray, suitable for mixing with flowers or other foliages. Most of the evergreens will hold for a month or longer in water without special treatment.

Sappy stems of conifers should be conditioned in cool water, as hot water encourages the sap to bleed; do not split the stems of coniferous plants. Other plant types benefit from having their stems split verti-cally with a cross cut and conditioning in hot water. Properly handled, evergreen foliage can be used again and again with different flowers. Be sure to recut the stems and use plenty of fresh, clean water to avoid a buildup of bacteria.

Consider some of the following for foliage accents in bouquets:

Aucuba japonica (golddust plant or Japanese aucuba)
Buxus (boxwood)
Euonymus (wintercreeper)
Ilex (holly)
Kalmia (mountain laurel)
Pachysandra (Japanese spurge)
Pinus (pines)
Rhododendron (rhododendron, azalea)
Thuja (arborvitae)
Tsuga (hemlock)

Almost all of the flowering shrubs offer something to the floral designer. Many of the spring bloomers can be forced for bloom indoors in the late winter; forsythia (*Forsythia × intermedia*) and flowering quince (*Chaenomeles japonica*) are two of the best. The summer bloomers will not force indoors in the summer because they bloom on new growth produced from the spring buds; butterfly bush (*Buddleia*) and hydrangea are two that fall into the summer category.

Harvest shrub flowers when they are fully developed and beginning to open up. Almost all types of woody plants will do best if all of the foliage is removed before conditioning. Condition stems in hot water after splitting the cut end of the stem with a cross cut. If you are having trouble conditioning a specific type of woody plant flower, consider placing the prepared stem in 2 inches of very hot—almost boiling—water for a few minutes before plunging them into a deep drink of warm water. If a specific stem still causes trouble, try shortening it. Extremely long stems are more difficult to condition than shorter stems. Allow woody plants to condition overnight before using them.

The following shrubs are good choices for harvesting for use in flower arrangements:

Abeliophyllum (white forsythia)
Amelanchier (shadblow)
Buddleia (butterfly bush)
Chaenomeles (flowering quince)
Deutzia (slender deutzia)
Forsythia (showy border forsythia)
Hydrangea (panicle, 'Peegee Hydrangea')
Kolkwitzia (beauty bush)
Philadelphus (mock orange)
Rhododendron (rhododendron, azalea)
Spiraea (spirea)
Syringa (lilac)
Viburnum (viburnum)
Weigela (weigela)

THE ROSE—QUEEN OF THE CUT FLOWERS

Rosa (ROE-sah) **rose**

Characteristics: The rose is revered in song and poem. Long the symbol of love, it has eased the way for many a heartsick young man. *Rosa* is a large genus of shrubs and has representatives from all over the world.

There are many types of roses suitable for the garden, but not all are good cutting roses. Some of the old-fashioned roses that perfume the air with their single blossoms will not last in water. Some of the very largest roses may be awkward and clumsy looking in a bouquet. Many of the newest rose introductions offer the gardener fragrance, beauty and improved hardiness and disease resistance.

For cutting, most of us are looking for roses that will produce cuttable stems and provide long-lasting blossoms. Hybrid Tea roses have long dominated the rose garden, prized for their beauty of form; range of color from white to deep red, yellow, orange and violet; and prolific flower production. Best picks from the Hybrid Tea group are 'Garden Party', a creamy white blushed with pale rose, 'Touch of Class', a delightful pink touched with coral, the rich, deeply red 'Chrysler Imperial', and the incomparably yellow 'Sunbright' and 'Lowell Thomas'. There are many Hybrid Tea roses, and any may make a worthy addition to the cutting garden.

Floribunda and Grandiflora roses combine Hybrid Tea purity of form with increased

Roses are ideal candidates for cutting from the garden. Varieties such as 'Gold Medal', a Grandiflora rose, are suitable for use singly in a bud vase or as sprays of roses in a larger arrangement of flowers.

'Red Meidiland' is one of a new generation of rose, combining the best of the modern roses with the scent, hardiness and vigor of old roses. These "shrub" roses are best cut and used in sprays.

The hybrid tea rose is the classic modern rose. Many new varieties such as 'Touch of Class' bring increased disease resistance to the garden.

Fresh roses from the garden. Cut roses should be plunged immediately into hot water in a clean container, to condition them before they are used in arrangements.

vigor and disease resistance. Consider 'Ivory Fashion' for bouquets; its creamy white blooms borne in clusters are very elegant. 'Queen Elizabeth' is a strong, medium pink Grandiflora. The Grandifloras have slightly smaller, single blooms on good cutting stems. The coral pink of 'Sonja' is considered one of the finest of the cutting roses offered in the commercial market and can be grown in the home cutting garden. 'Gold Medal' is a bright golden yellow Grandiflora.

For the floral designer, miniature roses may offer the largest group of roses superior in the vase as single blooms or sprays of multiple blooms. They range from tiny beauties that grow to 6 inches to varieties that produce smaller blossoms on stems to 3 to 4 feet in height. The flowers are an ideal size for use in bouquets of smaller flowers such as bachelor's buttons and *Nigella*. Miniature roses and sweetheart roses are usually grown on their own root stocks—they are not grafted—and offer superior hardiness to the Hybrid Teas, Floribundas and Grandifloras. 'Jean Kenneally' is a delightful apricot; 'Adam's Smile' is a blend of pink, yellow and coral, and 'Figurine' is a soft white rose with pink undertones. In the garden these roses will produce cuttable stems of a foot or more in length.

Shrub Roses are the roses of the future: tough, resilient, resistant to disease and hardy. Breeders are working to develop the traditional tough characteristics of the Shrub Roses with the everblooming qualities of the Hybrid Teas. The Meilland group of shrub roses are superior in all aspects: hardiness, fragrance, quality of bloom and reblooming ability.

Cultural Information: Roses should be planted in an area where they will receive a minimum 6 to 8 hours of sun per day. A southeastern exposure is ideal, providing adequate sunlight in the morning, yet protecting the shrubs from the hot sun of late afternoon. Roses tolerate a wide range of soil types. Paramount is soil drainage, which must be perfect. Prepare the soil deeply, incorporating peat moss or other organic matter that will improve the soil structure and nutrient-holding capacity of the soil.

Roses can be purchased as container-grown plants or bareroot nursery stock wrapped in fiber or moss. Soak bareroot plants in warm water overnight before planting. (Container-grown plants can be planted without soaking the roots.) Prune dormant plants back to 12 inches at the time of planting, cutting back to an outward-facing bud. Follow planting with a thorough watering and apply a 2- to 3-inch layer of organic mulch such as pine straw, cocoa shells, buckwheat hulls or ground corncobs. When roses begin to show growth, fertilize with a well-balanced, slow-release fertilizer such as 5-10-5. Repeat fertilizer applications when flowers start to open in June and again about 6 weeks later. Roses will flourish with adequate water during dry weather. Soaking the soil at the base of the roses is preferred to overhead irrigation, which can encourage disease.

Overwintering roses varies from region to region. In the Northeast, we usually apply a protective mulch around the base of the plants to cover the lower canes and, in grafted roses, the graft. Choose a mulching material that drains well so it doesn't hold moisture around the roots. After the plants are completely dormant in fall and the ground has started to freeze, apply the mulch in a cone-shaped mound over the crown of each plant. We frequently supplement this winter mulch with evergreen boughs that help hold the mulch in place and add extra insulation from winter winds, cold and the damage caused by alternate freezing and thawing. When the forsythia begins to bloom in spring, carefully remove the mulch from around the roses and spread it out over the surrounding soil to help conserve moisture and prevent weeds. For more information on overwintering, consult *Roses,* another book in the Burpee American Gardening Series.

Insects and disease can be a problem with roses, especially Hybrid Teas. By carefully choosing and preparing the site, maintaining good plant vigor, and selecting disease-resistant plants, we can do much to discourage disease. Cleanliness is critical with roses. Remove diseased leaves from the site and destroy them; do not add them to the compost heap. Organic, botanical and biological controls are available to combat many rose insects and diseases. *Harvest and Use:* Harvesting roses is, in fact, a pruning job. Roses should always be cut back to a bud just above a leaf with five or seven leaflets. Never prune back to a leaf with three leaflets as the growth resulting from that bud will, in all likelihood, be blind (will not produce a flower bud). Wherever possible, choose a bud that is facing out, away from the center of the plant. This pruning technique will encourage an open, uncluttered interior for the shrub. The rose shrub that is free from the clutter of many crossing branches and with an open habit will have better sun exposure and air circulation, and be less prone to disease.

Harvested roses should be stripped of any foliage that would sit under water and any thorns. The stems should be immediately placed in hot water for conditioning overnight. Roses treated in this way will last for 1 week or longer in fresh water. Roses can be enjoyed singly in bud vases, clustered with other flowers in a nosegay, or combined with lilies and delphiniums for an elegant centerpiece. Whatever the use, count on roses to provide unparalleled elegance of fragrance and form.

PLANTING LISTS FOR THE CUTTING GARDEN

FLOWERING TREES FOR THE CUTTING GARDEN

Many trees suitable for the small garden will produce flowers that will last well in water. In addition to fragrance and beauty of bloom, these trees may offer foliage, autumn color, ornamental fruits and twig formation. Consider incorporating one of the following trees in your landscape for cuttings.

Amelanchier laevis (shadblow)
Cercis canadensis (redbud)
Cornus spp. (dogwood)
Hamamelis virginiana (witch hazel)
Ilex spp. (holly)
Magnolia spp. (magnolia)
Malus spp. (apple, crabapple)
Oxydendrum arboretum (sorrel tree, sourwood)

Prunus spp. (cherry, plum, peach; ornamental and edible varieties)
Pyrus spp. (pear, ornamental pear)
Salix spp. (willow, pussy willow)
Tamarix (tamarisk, salt cedar)

FLOWERS FOR THE SHADY CUTTING GARDEN

ANNUALS

Ageratum houstonianum (blue flossflower)
Browallia speciosa (blush violet)
Coleus × hybridus (coleus)
Nicotiana spp. and hybrids (flowering tobacco)
Torenia fournieri (wishbone flower)
Tropaeolum majus (nasturtium)
Viola spp. (pansy, violet, Johnny-jump-up)

PERENNIALS

Aquilegia spp. and hybrids (columbine)
Astilbe spp. (false spirea)
Cimicifuga racemosa (black snakeroot)
Convallaria majus (lily of the valley)
Epimedium spp. (barrenwort)
Ferns (many genera)
Heuchera spp. (coralbells)
Hosta spp. and hybrids (plantain lily)

SHRUBS/GROUNDCOVERS

Enkianthus campanulatus (red-vein enkianthus)
Hedera helix (English ivy)
Kalmia latifolia (mountain laurel)
Pachysandra terminalis (pachysandra, Japanese spurge)
Rhododendron spp. (rhododendron, azalea)
Vinca minor (periwinkle)

WHITE FLOWERS FOR THE CUTTING GARDEN

ANNUALS

Antirrhinum majus (snap-dragon)*

Callistephus chinensis (China aster)*

Cosmos bipinnatus 'Sensation' (cosmos)*

Eustoma grandiflorum (lisian-thus, prairie gentian)*

Gomphrena globosa (globe amaranth)*

Gypsophila elegans (baby's breath)

Nicotiana spp. (flowering tobacco)*

Salvia farinacea 'Argent' (salvia)

Zinnia elegans (zinnia)*

PERENNIALS

Aquilegia spp. and hybrids (columbine)*

Astilbe spp. and hybrids (false spirea)*

Campanula spp. (bellflower)*

Chrysanthemum maximum (shasta daisy)

Convallaria majus (lily of the valley)

Echinacea purpurea 'White Star' (echinacea)

Gypsophila paniculata (baby's breath)

Hosta × 'Royal Standard' (hosta)

Paeonia lactifolia (peony)*

Phlox paniculata (garden phlox)*

Physostegia virginiana (obedi-ence plant)*

BULBS, CORMS, RHIZOMES AND TUBERS

Acidanthera bicolor (dark-eye gladixia)

Dahlia hybrids (garden dahlia)*

Gladiolus hybrids (gladiola)*

Narcissus spp. (narcissus, daffodil)*

Tulipa spp. (tulip)*

TREES AND SHRUBS

Deutzia gracilis (slender deutzia)*

Hydrangea paniculata (peegee hydrangea)

Kalmia latifolia (mountain laurel)*

Magnolia virginiana (sweetbay magnolia)*

Malus spp. (ornamental crab-apple)*

Oxydendron arboretum (sorrel tree)

Rhododendron spp. (rhododen-dron, azalea)*

Syringa vulgaris (lilac)*

*White flowers available as part of a seed mix of colors or by purchasing individually named varieties.

BLUE/LAVENDER FLOWERS FOR THE CUTTING GARDEN

ANNUALS

Ageratum houstonianum (blue flossflower)

Browallia speciosa (bush violet)

Callistephus chinensis (China aster)*

Centaurea cyanus (bachelor's button)*

Consolida orientalis (larkspur)*

Eustoma grandiflorum (lisian-thus, prairie gentian)*

Lathyrus odoratus (sweet pea)*

Matthiola incana (stock)*

Nigella damascena (love-in-a-mist)*

Salvia farinacea (mealycup sage, gentian sage)*

Scabiosa atropurpurea (pin-cushion flower)*

Trachelium caeruleum (purple umbrella)

Trachymene coerulea (blue lace flower)

Verbena bonariensis (verbena)

PERENNIALS

Aconitum napellus (monkshood)

Aquilegia × hybrida (col-umbine)*

Baptisia australis (false indigo)

*Blue or purple flowers available as part of a seed mix of colors or by purchasing individually named varieties.

Delphinium elatum (delphinium)
Hosta spp. (plantain lily)
Hyssopus officinalis (hyssop)
Iris spp. (iris)*
Lavandula angustifolia (lavender)

Nepeta spp. (catmint)
Phlox paniculata (garden phlox)*
Platycodon grandiflorus (balloonflower)*
Veronica spicata (speedwell)*
Viola spp. (garden violet)

BULBS, CORMS, RHIZOMES AND TUBERS

Allium spp. (allium, chive, onion)
Endymion hispanicus (wood hyacinth, Spanish squill)*
Gladiolus hybrids (gladiola)*
Tulipa hybrids (tulip)

*Blue or purple flowers available as part of a seed mix of colors or by purchasing individually named varieties.

YELLOW FLOWERS FOR THE CUTTING GARDEN

ANNUALS

Antirrhinum majus (snapdragon)*
Callendula officinalis (pot marigold)*
Celosia cristata (cockscomb)*
Cosmos sulphureus (Klondyke cosmos)*
Gaillardia pulchella (blanketflower)*
Helianthus annuus (sunflower)*
Hunnemannia fumariifolia (Mexican tulip poppy)
Tagetes spp. (marigold)*
Zinnia elegans (zinnia)*

PERENNIALS

Achillea spp. and hybrids (yarrow)*
Aquilegia × *hybrida* (columbine)*
Chrysanthemum × *morifolium* (hardy garden chrysanthemum)*
Coreopsis grandiflora (lance coreopsis)
Rudbeckia hirta (black-eyed Susan)
Solidago spp. (goldenrod)
Tanacetum vulgare (tansy)

BULBS, CORMS, RHIZOMES AND TUBERS

Dahlia hybrids (dahlia)*
Gladiolus hybrids (gladiola)*
Narcissus spp. (daffodil, narcissus)*
Tulipa spp. (tulip)*

TREES AND SHRUBS

Berberis vulgaris (common barberry)
Cytisus praecox (broom)
Forsythia × *intermedia* (showy border forsythia)
Hamamelis virginiana (common witch hazel)
Kerria japonica (Japanese kerria)*
Syringa vulgaris and hybrids (lilac)*

*Yellow flowers available as part of a seed mix of colors or by purchasing individually named varieties.

PINK AND RED FLOWERS FOR THE CUTTING GARDEN

ANNUALS

Amaranthus caudatus (love-lies-bleeding)

Antirrhinum majus (snapdragon)*
Callistephus chinensis (China aster)*

Celosia cristata and *C. plumosa* (cockscomb)*
Centaurea cyanus (bachelor's button)*

*Pink and red flowers available as part of a seed mix of colors or by purchasing individually named varieties.

Cosmos bipinnatus 'Sensation' (cosmos)*

Dianthus barbatus (sweet William)*

Eustoma grandiflorum (lisianthus, prairie gentian)*

Gomphrena globosa (globe amaranth)*

Lathyrus odoratus (sweet pea)*

Salvia splendens (garden sage)*

Scabiosa atropurpurea (pincushion flower)*

Xeranthemum annuum (immortelle)*

Zinnia elegans (zinnia)*

PERENNIALS

Aster spp. (Michaelmas daisy, aster)*

Astilbe spp. (false spirea)*

Chrysanthemum × morifolium (hardy garden chrysanthemum)*

Chrysanthemum coccineum (painted daisy)

Dianthus spp. (pinks)

Digitalis purpurea (foxglove)

Heuchera × hybrida (coralbells)

Liatris spicata (gayfeather)

Lilium spp. and hybrids (hardy lilies)*

Lychnis coronaria (rose campion, mullein pink)

Monarda didyma (bee balm)

Paeonia lactifolia (peony)*

Phlox paniculata (garden phlox)*

BULBS, CORMS, RHIZOMES AND TUBERS

Crocosmia spp. (montbretia)*

Dahlia hybrids (dahlia)*

Gladiolus hybrids (gladiola)*

Tulipa spp. and hybrids (tulip)*

TREES AND SHRUBS

Chaenomeles lagenaria (flowering quince)

Hydrangea paniculata grandiflora (peegee hydrangea)

Kalmia latifolia (mountain laurel)

Malus spp. (flowering crabapple)

Prunus spp. (ornamental cherry)

Rhododendron spp. (rhododendron, azalea)*

Syringa spp. (lilac)*

*Pink and red flowers available as part of a seed mix of colors or by purchasing individually named varieties.

ORANGE, RUSSET AND BROWN FLOWERS FOR THE CUTTING GARDEN

ANNUALS

Amaranthus caudatus (love-lies-bleeding)

Antirrhinum majus (snapdragon)*

Calendula officinalis (pot marigold)*

Celosia cristata and C. plumosa (cockscomb)*

Cosmos sulphureus (Klondyke cosmos)*

Gomphrena globosa (globe amaranth)*

Helianthus annuus (sunflower)

Reseda odorata (mignonette)

Zinnia elegans (zinnia)*

PERENNIALS

Chrysanthemum × morifolium (hardy garden chrysanthemum)

Gaillardia × grandiflora (blanketflower)

Rudbeckia hirta (gloriosa daisy)

BULBS, CORMS, RHIZOMES AND TUBERS

Crocosmia spp. (montbretia)*

Dahlia hybrids (dahlia)*

Lilium spp. and hybrids (hardy lilies)*

Gladiolus hybrids (gladiola)*

Tulipa spp. and hybrids (tulip)*

*Orange, russet or brown flowers available as part of a seed mix of colors or by purchasing individually named varieties.

Appendix

THE USDA PLANT HARDINESS MAP OF THE UNITED STATES

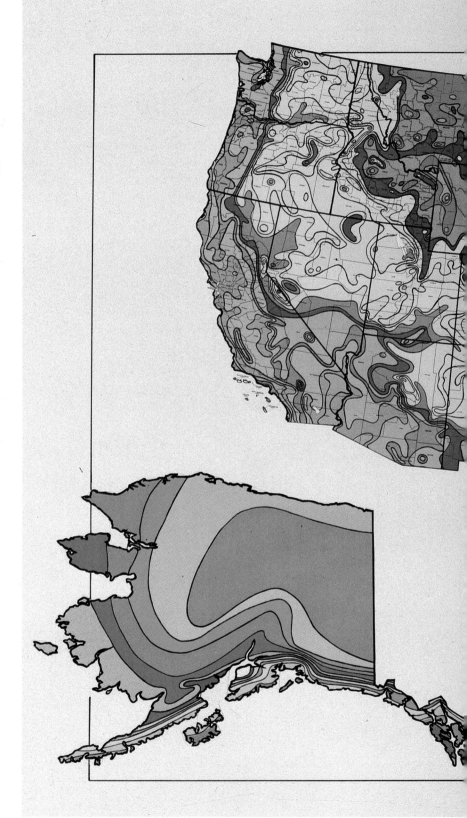

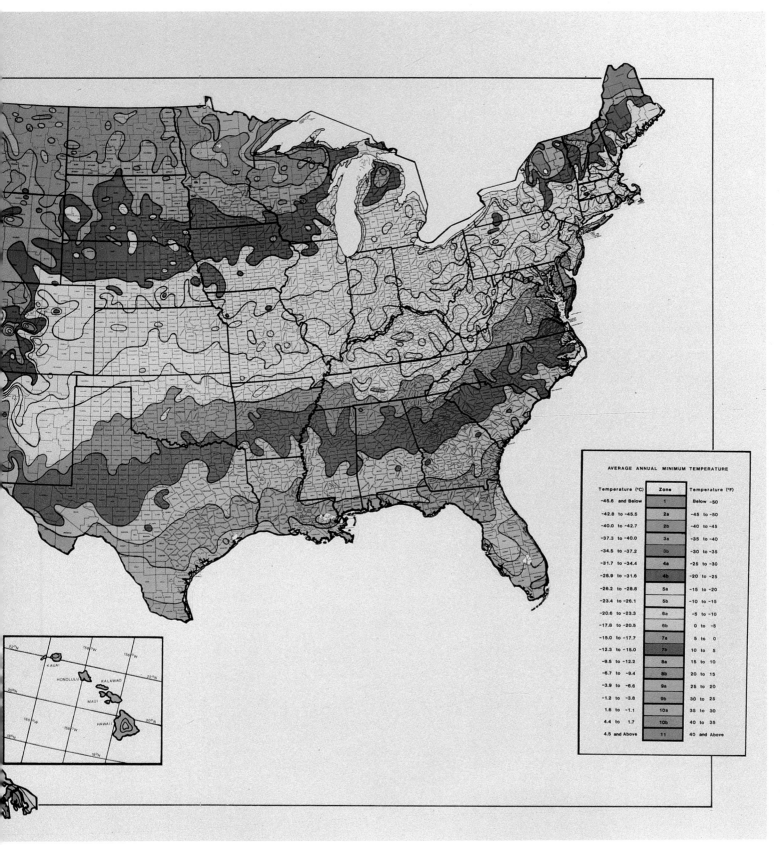

AVERAGE ANNUAL MINIMUM TEMPERATURE

Temperature (°C)	Zone	Temperature (°F)
-45.6 and Below	1	Below -50
-42.8 to -45.5	2a	-45 to -50
-40.0 to -42.7	2b	-40 to -45
-37.3 to -40.0	3a	-35 to -40
-34.5 to -37.2	3b	-30 to -35
-31.7 to -34.4	4a	-25 to -30
-28.9 to -31.6	4b	-20 to -25
-26.2 to -28.8	5a	-15 to -20
-23.4 to -26.1	5b	-10 to -15
-20.6 to -23.3	6a	-5 to -10
-17.8 to -20.5	6b	0 to -5
-15.0 to -17.7	7a	5 to 0
-12.3 to -15.0	7b	10 to 5
-9.5 to -12.2	8a	15 to 10
-6.7 to -9.4	8b	20 to 15
-3.9 to -6.6	9a	25 to 20
-1.2 to -3.8	9b	30 to 25
1.6 to -1.1	10a	35 to 30
4.4 to 1.7	10b	40 to 35
4.5 and Above	11	40 and Above

(NOTE: Italized page numbers refer to captions)

Cut along dotted line.

Burpee American Gardening Series Readers:

Save $3.00
with This Exclusive Offer!

There are lots of good reasons why thousands of gardeners order their seeds, bulbs, plants and other gardening supplies from the Burpee Gardens Catalogue: highest quality products, informed and courteous service, and a guarantee on which you can depend.

Now there's another good reason: you can save $3.00 on an order of $10.00 or more from the 1994 Burpee Gardens Catalogue. This is an exclusive offer available only to readers of the Burpee American Gardening Series. Just enclose this coupon with your order and deduct $3.00 from the total where indicated on the order form from your catalogue.
If you need a Catalogue just send in the coupon below.

Your signature _____

This discount coupon must accompany your order. **Offer expires 12/31/94.**

This offer is not transferable. No photocopies or facsimiles of the coupon will be accepted. Coupon has no cash value and may not be redeemed for cash or exchanged for products at retail stores. Offer void where prohibited, taxed or otherwise restricted.

Cut along dotted line.

FREE!
Gardening's Most Wanted Catalogue!

Start your garden or expand it with high quality products from Burpee. The 1994 Burpee Gardens Catalogue features seeds, bulbs and plants for new varieties of flowers and vegetables as well as hundreds of old favorites and a broad range of garden supplies.
 Send in this coupon today to:

W. Atlee Burpee & Company
000646 Burpee Building
Warminster, PA   18974

Please send me a free 1994 Burpee Gardens Catalogue.

Name _____

Street _____

City _____ State _____ Zip _____

000646